On the Street Doing Life

The West Side of Chicago through the Eyes of a cop called "Cronie"

Anne Keegan

Bloomington, IN Milton Keynes, UK

authorHOUSE®

AuthorHouse™
1663 Liberty Drive, Suite 200
Bloomington, IN 47403
www.authorhouse.com
Phone: 1-800-839-8640

AuthorHouse™ UK Ltd.
500 Avebury Boulevard
Central Milton Keynes, MK9 2BE
www.authorhouse.co.uk
Phone: 08001974150

First published by AuthorHouse 1/16/2007

ISBN: 978-1-4259-8976-7 (sc)

Library of Congress Control Number: 2007900102

Printed in the United States of America
Bloomington, Indiana

This book is printed on acid-free paper.

DEDICATION

Left to Right: Grapes, Drozd, Cronie, Sergeant Connelly, Babyface

This book is dedicated to a unique team of policemen who worked in the gang unit on the West Side of Chicago. For recent decades, it was one of the most dangerous neighborhoods in the world. Yet these men loved their work and seldom got discouraged.

Cast of Characters:

There was their "Sarge," grizzled in looks but gentlemanly in manner,

Sgt. Gene Connelly.

And his crew:

Grapes- Bob Grapenthein
Babyface- John Rawski
Drozd- Bobby Drozd
Cronie- Mike Cronin, the cop with only one foot.

Also, this is dedicated to the troubled and tormented souls trapped in this urban ghetto, especially the "little girl with a hole in her heart."

This is a collection of portraits revealing the humanity on the West Side as witnessed by these policemen who day after day dealt with it.

TABLE of CONTENTS

PREFACE

There's nothing easy about the West Side of Chicago. It is alert even when it sleeps. It is tense even when it naps. Early mornings are not soft, they are simply empty. Twilight does not come gentle, like a balm for what has been that day but more as an anxious portent of what will come that night.

"The West Si-I-I-I-de." There is a rhythm to the way you say it, letting the last word slide. There is a rhythm to the way life ebbs and flows here, different from the rest of the city, as if life here is determined by the spell of a separate moon, with its own tides. They walk a little different and talk a little different out here.

West Siders can spot each other anywhere. It is a small town inside a big city. This part of town wakes up when the rest of the city shuts down and goes to sleep. And it sleeps when the rest of the city is bleary and catching the morning bus.

It has hard working people and down home grandmothers from the South with grandchildren lost to the corner life. It has drug dealers, old time junkies, forgotten musicians, unpublished poets, too many unwed mothers and desperate teenagers. It has absent fathers, illiterate high school drop-outs who will never hold a job in their lives and hucksters of all kinds. It has produced kids who somehow have gone somewhere--on to college and luckily escaped--and then thousands who have gone nowhere, lost in the morass of the streets. It has a sense of humor, a natural ability to laugh from deep down inside and not care about tomorrow. It also has a violent temper triggered by dark repressions. It can dance all night and sleep til noon. It can weep and mourn and then soon, forget.

If the West Side could be embodied in the soul of a man, he'd gamble and take his losses without crying; he'd smoke a good cigar on his last three bucks and he'd give you a wink when he passed you on the street.

The West Side has one of the highest concentrated crime rates in the world. It contains one of the busiest and most violent police districts in Chicago. It is an old time district that used to be called Fillmore. Still is. But the official name is now Harrison. This is where a young policeman named Mike Cronin wanted to work when he got out of the academy more than three decades ago. And this is where he went and happily stayed. He got to know the broken curbs of every drug corner and which buildings had back steps that creaked. He got people to tell him things they never thought they'd tell a cop. He'd pop up in the grimy corridors of the projects just when everyone thought the police shift was over. He knew what basements were rented out as "smoke houses" and made frequent visits. He'd seen men grow rich off drugs and bodies found crumpled cold from overdoses. Over time, Cronin has seen change and yet nothing has changed, like the turn of seasons that come back upon themselves. Names change. Faces change. And ages, they get younger. But little else.

He's become as familiar a figure on the street as the people who live here. One old timer said it straight while sitting in the back of Cronin's squad car. They had played cat and mouse for years these two, cop and junkie.

"Yo!" said Cronin, talking to the old timer, "You still here? Man, you're on the street do'in life!"

"Yeah," chuckled the old timer, "same as you Cronie, just the same as you."

VIETNAM, THE DOUBLE BUBBLE AND A MASS CARD FOR THE 'OLD MAN'

In St. Gertrude's parish, where he grew up, the other kids had their own street name for him. They called him 'Sam'. No one is sure why but that one fits too. His mother, Mae, an Irish immigrant from County Antrim in Northern Ireland, always called him 'Michael' with a certain velvet lift to the way she said the word.

He was named after his father, a County Kerry man, whom everyone called 'Mike."In the neighborhood where he lived, seven miles north of downtown Chicago, just about everyone was Catholic, many were Irish, and nobody owned their own house. They lived in big apartments, along with lots of kids, not enough bedrooms, small kitchens, one bathroom and fathers who left for work early in the morning, carrying their lunch. This was meat and potatoes, green beans and corn-from-a-can-for-supper country. This is when you still said grace at dinner and waited for your father to pick up his fork before you dove into the potatoes. This is where you ate hot oatmeal for breakfast, fought with your sisters to get into the bathroom, walked to school (nobody was bussed) and if you were in trouble with the nuns in class, God help you, because the nuns were right. And the priest was righter.

This is where your mother stayed home to run the house and your father worked overtime and on his days off so the tuition at Catholic school could get paid for you and your brothers and sisters. This is where you could reach out and tap the window of the apartment glass next door. Where laundry went up on sunny days in the back

1

yard propped up by poles, and the ladies chatted among themselves across fences because they had everything in common. This was back when a family outing was taken by bus or trolley and you didn't stay overnight. Cronin's father, an employee of the Chicago Transit Authority, proudly drove an el train but never learned how to drive a car or had a driver's license. And that made sense to him. The Cronins didn't own a car.

This was a part of urban America that no longer exists, urban villages, singular ethnic patches, that made up the quilt of Chicago before the great exodus out of town, over the city limits and into a burgeoning suburbia that ended it all. This is where the landlord and his wife lived above you and told on you if you were acting up on the corner or broke the fence gate or picked Mrs. Hanratty's tomatoes while they were still green and splatted them against a neighbor's garage wall.

This is where everyone went to mass on Sunday and people ate Sunday dinner before 4 p.m., the dishes done and the kitchen swept by 5. None of the dads owned golf clubs and nobody's older brother was on a tennis team. These were the times when grandma settled in with the family once she became a widow, you shared a double bed with your brother, fought for the open window side on a hot August night and kept turning the pillow over in the middle of the night, looking for the cool part.

This was a place of yesteryear. Crowded, blue collar, but not poor. Clean, thrifty, with a savings account but not much in it. No stocks and bonds portfolios for dad. The stock was put into the kids so they'd have it better. It was a society strict but not unforgiving. Good natured but not incapable of frowning and giving you a good swat. It was a world where fathers belonged to unions and mothers wore aprons. Where boys could come home with a shiner as long as they hadn't gotten arrested and girls could stay out until midnight as long at they stayed in the neighborhood and their older brother was watching who they were flirting with.

This is where there was always someone in the family who was a priest or a nun working in South America and your aunts sent them money at Christmas time. Where it was understood you'd finish high school, even if you hated it and you made it through with a quiet prayer in English and a D in Latin -- but you made it.

This was a Chicago neighborhood where your mom shopped at the local stores along Devon Avenue, your dad drank at his favorite corner tavern and everyone went to silver anniversary parties in the church basement. Back then, in Chicago, neighborhoods were defined by what parish you lived in, even when you weren't Catholic.

And this is how Cronin grew up, among tight families and unbreakable loyalties among friends. He was 'Sam' from St. Gertrude's and he got into his share of fights over the fact because the boys from St. Gertrude's were no angels. Far from it. Even after high school, they were a baseball team -- "The Playboys." They were a football team, "The Monaco Colts." They were a clan, and everyone on the north side knew it. When the Colts played the prisoners at Indiana State Prison in football, they got into a melee with the prisoners, the game was stopped, the yards were locked down, and the boys from St. Gertrude's were thrown out and never invited back again. They were the only team to ever be thrown out of prison. They took pride in that. The team from St. Gertrude's figured they won, no matter the score.

Cronin played an enthusiastic role in all of this. It wasn't that Cronin was the biggest or the fastest and always won a brawl, but his stubbornness made him tough and his inability to admit defeat made him formidable. Nobody ever wanted to fight him, not because they couldn't fell him once or even twice, – he was a short, stocky little guy – but because he'd stagger back up and go at it again and never give up. His contentious Irish genes were his strongest asset. He was like the rest of them. Young and strong and crazy and let his muscles do his thinking.

He came from a family of five children, two sisters, two brothers, and he – the chubby one with blond hair – was the next to the last. His brother, Jimmy, came six years later. At St. Gertrude's, where he went to grammar school, he always was one of the first to flunk out of the spelling bee, then sit down in his desk and take a nap. Bored, of course, pretending that he didn't care.

Only as an adult did he realize that he was probably dyslexic and dyslexia was the last thing the B.V.M. nuns had their eye out for. But he could see clear enough to catch a ball and was the first to join a sports team, and all through St. Gertrude's and DePaul Academy for high school, he was athletic and he and the other boys played a game of anything wherever there was an open lot or empty playground. He ended up on the All City Catholic football team of 1962. He played guard. And like everyone else, he stayed pretty much in his own neighborhood and close to home. Even after graduation from high school, they all lived at home. He and his buddies drank quarts of Budweiser at the Foster Avenue Beach after work, worked blue collar jobs, and waited for their dreams to happen.

For many of them, the dream was to become a cop. It was for Cronin. He and his best friend, Jerry Hanrahan, were going to do it together. Jerry's dad was a cop. His two older brothers were going to be cops. But in the late sixties, boys from St. Gertrude's, who didn't have college deferrals or fathers who could pick up a phone and call a state senator to ask a favor, got drafted. They were all young men who got a job the day after they graduated from Catholic high school and were waiting to become cops or firemen or iron workers. And then Vietnam got hot and one by one, before they could get married and have kids, and become exempt, they all got letters from Uncle Sam to report downtown at the recruitment center. They were all healthy and in good shape and so, if ya got to go, join the Marines, and Semper Fi, put a star in the window, mom, I'll be back soon.

First Jimmy Lyons went and then Jimmy Blomstrand and Mike Brown and Don Karolick, Bobby Hanrahan and finally Bobby's younger brother, Jerry -- the kid from the neighborhood that Cronin loved best. One by one, Cronin's buddies from the neighborhood left for the service. He watched them go and the neighborhood fall empty. He'd share beers with them on their last night on leave and he'd see them off the next day at the train, shaking their hands with that innocence and lack of nostalgia young men have when they part for the first time--good time Charlie hand shakes and I'll-see-you-again-soon slaps on the back.

It didn't bother Cronin. He'd weighed in at 20 pounds overweight and been labeled 4F. So he didn't have to get sent to some forlorn rice paddy in Southeast Asia to fight a war he didn't understand. He was the lucky one. Besides, the guys would all be back soon, out of uniform, playing pick-up ball, meeting at the Double Bubble Saloon and dropping by the house at night. Everything would be the same again. But it never is. And it wasn't for Mike Cronin.

Word came soon that Jerry Hanrahan had been killed in action, on Hill 881 North, in the Republic of South Vietnam on April 30, 1967 near the DMZ. A bullet from a 50 caliber machine gun had crashed through his chest and into his heart and ended his young life before it had ever really begun. The word came with the ring of a door bell. Kitty Hanrahan, his little sister, then 17, answered the door. A Marine was standing there, formal and uncomfortable with what he had to say. She took one look at the stranger in uniform and just knew. Before he could utter a word she quietly closed the door in his face and walked back into the kitchen, pretending that death was not at their doorstep, waiting to ring the bell again.

"Who was at the door?" asked her mother.

"Nobody," said Kitty and she sat down at the kitchen table. Then the bell rang again.

"I thought you said there was nobody at the door," said Mrs. Hanrahan.

"Go see, Kitty, please."

Kitty opened the door and the Marine was still there as unmovable as a tombstone. She left the door open without inviting him in, left him standing there and then came back to her mother and said,

"There's a Marine at the door."

"Oh, it must be a friend of Jerry's," said Mary Hanrahan, smiling, and she got up from her chair, walked to the door and invited the young man in. Kitty ran into the bathroom where her brother, Bobby, who was just back from the service, was slicking back his dark hair with a wet comb.

"Bobby, there's a Marine at the door and he wants to talk to mom," she said.

"Oh shit," said Bobby and he put down the comb.

Kitty ran out the bathroom, past the marine who was just sitting down, through the apartment, out the front door and directly across the street over to St. Gertrude's church. She tugged on both of the large wooden doors but they were locked. Even the church could give her no escape from that which she didn't want to know. Trembling, she returned to her house where the marine was now sitting at the kitchen table. Her mother was no longer smiling. The visitor was not a friend of Jerry's on leave stopping by the house to say hello. He was a Marine with a terrible assignment. He'd come to tell the family that Jerry was dead.

Jerry Hanrahan was not just any kid from the neighborhood. He was president of his senior class at St. Patrick's High School, captain of the football team and he had a girl a few blocks over, a beautiful girl, Patty Mulvaney, waiting to marry him when he came home. He was a golden boy with promise. Now suddenly word had come that he died far away on a beat up, blown up, blasted away hill near an Asian village no one in the neighborhood had ever heard of in a war none of them understood.

The young men in the neighborhood who'd never cried, cried openly and the girls, who always cried, tried not to. Either way, the neighborhood called St. Gertrude's parish was in despair. Before his body was returned, Patty Mulvaney went to the Double Bubble Saloon, where everyone their age went, to find someone to talk to. She walked in alone and sat on a stool at the end of the bar and began to cry. Billy Heavey, not that much older than her but already married, leaned down to console her. He was working a second job as the night bar tender. She had Jerry's engagement ring that he bought her, she told him. But she'd never bought a ring for Jerry. She'd been waiting to buy it when he came home. Now he was coming home and she had nothing to put on his finger. Nothing to show that they loved each other very much and were going to be married. She began to sob. Without pausing for a second, Billy Heavey took off his own wedding ring, handed it to her and said, "Give this to Jerry." And at the funeral home, when his young body was returned, she slipped it on his finger.

The wake was at the Barr Funeral Home on Broadway and that Friday evening in May Cronin walked in with his buddy, Jimmy Lyons. Both were to be pallbearers the next morning at the funeral. They stopped, as they entered the crowded room, to talk to Kitty and in a moment of grief, she said something she shouldn't but that she felt.

"I wish it was you that died," she said, "and not my brother."

Then she ran into the bathroom, locked the door and wept into a wad of toilet paper that muffled her sobs and absorbed the tears. She didn't mean it. But she didn't want Jerry dead either.

The funeral was on Saturday, May 13th and the Chicago Daily News devoted almost a whole page to the death of Jerry Hanrahan. He had become the 373rd boy from Chicago to die in Vietnam. Veteran reporter Ed Rooney began his story like this:

> *"Pat Mulvaney, 20, sobbed softly as she walked behind the flag draped casket. Her diamond engagement ring sparkled for a moment in the May sunlight. Eight young men, several in tears, slowly eased the steel-encased burden into the vestibule of St. Gertrude's Church at 1420 West Granville Avenue. Pat Mulvaney's fiancee, US Marine Corporal Jerome M. Hanrahan, Jr. was back from Hill 881, Vietnam. They had planned to marry next February at St. Gertrude's...*

> *"Who was Jerry Hanrahan? You could have seen him during the 20 years or so that he spent here in his native city. You might have glanced at a sandy haired, 8 year old tugging on his mother's arm while Christmas shopping in the Loop. You might have spotted a classy high school football quarterback in Hansen Park. Or paid a bill to a courteous young man in a cashier's cage at People's Gas."*

The story ended as it began--with the neighborhood girl who loved him.

> *"'Regrets, no,' she answered. 'I was lucky to have known him and loved him. We are all proud that he died fighting for his country.'"*

Within three months, Cronin quit his job at the CTA screwing bolts into elevated train cars and announced he was joining the

Marine Corps. His father stated at dinner that he thought the move was unwise--giving up a fine job with the city to join the Marines when he didn't have to.

Kitty Hanrahan and Patty Mulvaney, badly bruised from Jerry's death and knowing now that neighborhood heroes do not always march off in uniform and come home in one piece, begged him not to do it. But his mind was set. Out of guilt, out of pride, and out of a deep and resolute despair, Cronin vowed privately to avenge the death of his best friend.

"I think he felt that if he couldn't get the one who killed Jerry then he'd go and get them all," says Kitty.

That fall he and Jimmy Lyons climbed into Cronin's '65 Pontiac GTO and drove to California. Once they got there, Cronin sold the car, went on a diet, lost the 20 pounds that had made him 4F and then the two of them knocked on the door of a recruiter and joined the Marines. Both of them said they wanted to go to Vietnam. The Marines granted their wish. On September 25, 1968 Cronin landed in Danang.

He'd never been colder in his life. It was the rainy season when he trooped down the steps of the plane and onto the tarmac. The Marines had no spare ponchos to give to the new men and they were all drenched within ten minutes and stayed that way. They sat like dummy's in ditches and got soaked day after day waiting to be dispatched. They never dried out. After two days of being wet and never dry and always cold at night and not wanting to be stuck in a mortar company anyway, Cronin asked to do something less passive and more active. This wasn't kicking ass and that's what he came for. This was stupid. Put him in the front lines, he asked. And again, like the magic genie the Marine Corp can be, they granted his wish within five days.

> "Dear Mr. and Mrs. Cronin:" said the form letter dated September 30, 1968-- their names typed in with a faded and overused light grey ink ribbon.
> "I should like to take this opportunity to introduce myself as your son's new commanding officer and to explain briefly what his duties will be while a member of this command ...Your son will be assigned to a

Combined Action Platoon (CAP). A CAP is the joining of U.S. Marines and local Vietnamese militia, called Popular Forces, to form a village security force.

"This force consists of 35 Vietnamese Popular Force soldiers, a 14 man Marine rifle squad and one Navy corpsman. The Popular Force personnel are local villagers armed, equipped and trained primarily for the role of village security.

"The marines act as military advisors and provide the experience and know-how for adequate village security. A most important member of this team, the corpsman, provides medical aid to Marines, Popular Forces and local villagers alike.

"As the CAP trains, works and conducts counter-guerilla operations, the Vietnamese contingent becomes more proficient and is finally capable of assuming full responsibility for the mission of insuring the security of their village.

"The squad leader has trained his counterpart and the individual Marine has assisted in instilling the team spirit in the PF. The corpsman, likewise, has brought one or more Vietnamese to an acceptable level of medical proficiency.

"With this accomplished, the Marines are then able to move on to another village which does not enjoy the freedom from Viet Cong harassment, and the cycle begins again. This is the program your son will be associated with for the remainder of his tour in Vietnam. It is an important program, they depend upon him for their freedom to live free of Viet Cong reprisals, to harvest their rice without enemy taxation and to send their children to school each day knowing the teacher was not kidnaped or murdered during the night. A more fulfilling mission could be found nowhere in Vietnam today."

It was signed, *"E.F. Pierson, Lt. Colonel, U.S. Marine Corps".*

What Cronin liked best about being in a CAP unit was being out in the little villages--freer to move about and interact with the locals than he would had he been   assigned to a mortar company.

"Now Michael," wrote his mother from home. "Are you going to mass on Sunday or do you ever see a priest?"

"Mom," he wrote back, "Out here we don't see anyone."

The three villages 40 miles outside of Chu Lai that his patrol was assigned to is where Cronin stayed for five months and 25 days. They lived in bunkers and dined on C-rations, surrounded by a wall of sandbags. Cronin never got to go on R and R. But one day, unannounced, a helicopter came thawack-wack-wacking in low, blowing up dust and roof thatch, scattering squawking chickens and bending bamboo trees to the ground and dropped one case of Budweiser to the men. It was the Marine Corps' birthday. Happy Birthday and they waved adios. Then the chopper rose straight up into the low clouds, hit the forward button and disappeared. Cronin doesn't think he drank one beer. It was hot enough to have a cool one but too hot to drink a warm one. They gave their beer away.

He went on 110 patrols and ambushes while he was out in the bush. The raids they conducted were usually done at dawn and often the Popular Forces turned and ran if the fighting got too heavy. He remembers bringing in a group of Vietnamese prisoners they'd taken and turning them over to the Popular Forces for questioning. One half hour later, one of the prisoners floated by him while he was on patrol along the ocean. The prisoner was face up and very dead. A week later, inside their compound, Cronin watched the Vietnamese PF colonel start to torture a local villager. Cronin, who was only a private, walked over and told the Colonel, to stop it. Outraged, the Colonel pulled his pistol and pointed it at Cronin.

"I mean it," said Cronin and he slapped the Colonel's face.

Stunned, the colonel let go of the villager's shirt and released him. Cronin walked away.

On December 8, three days before his 25th birthday, while on routine patrol along a soft white beach just 50 yards from the South China Sea, while the midday sun was burning hot on his shoulders and an afternoon quiet had settled over the baked sand, Mike Cronin stepped on a booby trap and lost most of his left foot.

The kid next to him stepped on one first. His boot came down on a mine hidden carefully under the sand and in one wild explosion of sand and dust and bone and blood, the young Marine walking next to him was thrown into the air and fell dying in the heat beside him. That explosion blinded Cronin and he staggered sightless down the beach, lost and stumbling, until his left boot hit something hard and metallic under the sand and with a second roar from the ground, he was thrown into the air and then collapsed, his foot in shreds.

He lay there bleeding for a long time. He doesn't know how long for pain loses the perspective of time. There were a lot of voices shouting over his head and he could hear the radio crackling and a buddy calling for help. He remembers the sun searing down on his pain and he couldn't see and nobody could help him and he lay there writhing in the burning sand. Contrary to the letter the lieutenant colonel had written his parents about the importance of the Navy corpsman, there was no corpsman in his platoon. They had not been up to strength for months so there was no one to even give him morphine while he lay and bled into his shattered boot and the boot, with the bottom blown off, let his blood ooze out and create its own small ruddy pond on the beach. The corpsman who came to tend Cronin was flown in by helicopter from a Navy ship off the coast.

When they picked him up and moved him to a stretcher, they looked down where he'd been lying and winced. For he'd landed, when he collapsed, on another land mine that had failed to go off. He was given morphine, an IV and MEDIVACed to DaNang. There a young nurse leaned over him and asked him if he had been given anything for the pain. Cronin lied and said, "No."

So they gave him more and the pain began to lighten him onto almost a cloud of ecstacy. Then they bandaged his blind eyes, stopped the bleeding in his left foot and a priest came to his side and held his arm and gave him the last rights. Before he faded out, he asked someone if he would ever see again. Would he be blind? A male voice told him it would take some time to know, they'd sutured up the cornea in his left eye. Then the voice told him they were going to have to take off his left foot.

And he begged them, "God, please don't do that." I'm going to be a policeman and I need two feet."

And then he passed out and woke up in a Navy hospital in Tokyo. He still had his foot, though he could not see it. The bandages over his eyes had not yet been removed but the nurses told him it was still there and he believed them.

Five days later, they took the bandages off his eyes and his vision was there, though not perfect at first. And his eyes hurt. Now again they told him they'd have to amputate his foot. His answer was the same. He said no, he would not sign the amputation papers. He was going to become a policeman and in Chicago policemen need two feet.

They shipped him next to the Naval Hospital in Memphis, Tennessee. He arrived on a C-130 along with scores of other broken young bodies, brought in on stretchers with IV bottles swaying from poles, still groggy from morphine, confused by the flight, unable to understand that parts of their body would never be the same. And scared.

"We always knew when they were coming in and when they came in, they came in batches and we'd do triage," remembers Dr. Richard Greenberg of North Easton, Massachusetts, who was a young lieutenant and a surgeon in the orthopedic ward of the hospital the day Cronin arrived . "I had a lot of faith in those guys. They'd gone through hell, came in all beat up and had to go through hell again just to get back to where they were before the war and that's all they were asking for. Their spirit was wonderful. We had one kid who went horseback riding with two casts on his legs.

"And another who came in with bones shattered in both legs and filled with open wounds and infection and all we could do is slap casts on him and then get him up and make him walk. And he got up on those casts and took a step and broke down and started to cry from happiness because he thought he'd never walk again."

Cronin arrived there on December 19, 1968 with fragment wounds to the right eye, his left hand and left foot. "Viability and usefulness of the foot was questionable," his medical report said. "The patient had a markedly infected left foot which was draining obvious purulent material and, after removal of the sutures in the foot done previously in Danang, large amounts of pus egressed from the interior of the foot."

Immediately, upon entry into the hospital, four foreign bodies, one steel and three sand were removed from his left eye. Two days later, more sand and metal were taken out of his right eye. It was also decided that the patient would have to lose his foot--gangrene was setting in and if Cronin held out any longer, he could die. A priest came to his bedside and asked if he would like to take confession before they operated.

"Well, father," said Cronin, "it's not as if I've been to any wild parties lately."

On Christmas Eve, 1968, they cut off Mike Cronin's left foot. He was awake during the amputation and could hear the sound of the saw. That night he complained of being cold and they gave him blankets. His temperature rose to 105.8 and he was given more blood and constant rubdowns with alcohol and ice. The nurse noted in her report that "the patient is very annoyed with his condition." That Christmas Day was a blur to him. It was not joyful and he prefers not to remember it.

For two weeks after the operation, Cronin had a high fever that would not go down, rising up to 104 during the day and down to 100 at night. The dressings on his leg were changed every day. Three days after the amputation he was given two more units of packed red cells.

Over the New Year's holiday, his mother and his two sisters came down from Chicago to visit him.

"If you could've seen his face, poor boy lying there, you wouldn't give a nickel for him," remembers his mother. "He was in so much pain.

"I asked to talk to a doctor and when I went into his office, he said, 'Do you want me to do the talking or do you want to ask the questions?' And I said, 'Doctor, I just want to know how my son is.' And he said, 'Well, I'm not optimistic'."

Despite a persistent fever, Cronin's leg began to heal. After several weeks, and a second operation to take more of the foot off, they had him up on crutches and walking around. By March 1 they had him on a hospital plane heading north and sent him to Hines Veteran's Hospital in Maywood, just outside of Chicago. There he was put in an amputation ward to wait to be fitted for his prosthesis while the stump of his leg, amputated just above the ankle, healed itself. He was surrounded by boys missing arms, missing legs, missing everything, missing out on life. Each evening, once the lights were out and the big ward fell quiet he could hear a kid a few beds down begin to cry and call out for his mother in the dark. He'd been a door gunner on a helicopter gun ship and when it got hit by a mortar and exploded, he was the only one who fell to the earth alive. He had no arms and no legs and was blind. He was only 19 and Cronin never knew his name. But he and everyone else on the ward closed their eyes every night and listened to him weep.

There was another vet he'd talk to, a Sluggo type from Michigan. He'd been a truck driver before the war and now was blind.

"I know where I'm going when I go back home and I'm going to stay there," the guy told him bitterly. "Third bar stool on the left at a tavern I know just outside of Detroit," he'd say. "I'll find that stool with my cane, sit down and spend the rest of my life there. That's where I'll be, forever, I guess."

Cronin wanted out of there. He wanted to go home. He didn't need to be taking up a bed when he could get around on crutches. He didn't want to hear any more of this. He didn't want to see it. He didn't want to smell that hospital elixir of medicine, antiseptic, urine and whatever they used twice a day to mop the floors. He was sick of nurses and doctors and being told what to do and of lying in bed and people feeling sorry for him.

He was sick of being sick. So Cronin went home to the second floor apartment on Glenwood Avenue. Back to the familiar. To St. Gertrude's and the old neighborhood. Once there, he'd figure something out, somehow. He'd have to. Because all he knew now was that at 25 he was suddenly a handicapped vet with one foot, a pair of crutches and no idea what he was going to do for the rest of his life. The only thing he knew for sure was that he could never become a policeman. Not ever.

On crutches, it was a long walk to the Double Bubble Saloon over on Broadway. In the spring of 1969 he broke four sets of crutches hobbling along that mile stretch to the neighborhood tavern each night where all his friends hung out. He started going every night. And more than once, after a few beers, he'd sit at the bar with his head down, feeling nothing but sorry for himself. There was nothing much else left to feel. His best friend was dead, his dream of being a cop was over, his left foot was gone and Jimmy, his little brother, had been drafted and was over in Vietnam.

"I saw him there one night with his face hanging down into his beer and said, 'Come on, Sam. I'll drive you home,'" remembers Kitty Hanrahan. "And he let me. My boy friend, Denny, and I let him out of the car and he went up into his apartment without saying anything and he closed the door and Denny said, 'He didn't protest enough about being brought home. I bet right now he is sneaking out the back door'. So we drove around into the alley and there was Sam heading back to the tavern.

"I got out of the car and said, 'Sam, you've had enough to drink. Go back in the house.' He staggered a second and looked at me and said, 'You don't know.' And I said, 'I don't know what Sam?'"

"'You just don't know,' he said again.

"'What don't I know?' I asked again.

" 'You don't know what it's like to have a brother in Vietnam,' he said.

"'I don't?' I said, starting to shout. 'I only had one killed there, Sam! What's wrong with you'?"

"Then he looked at me real deep, like he was just seeing for the first time who he was talking to and he said, 'Oh my God. What did I say? 'And I said, 'Get in that house right now. If you don't go in and stay there, there will be no mercy for you in the hereafter, I'm telling ya.

"And he went slowly up the back steps, closed the door and stayed there."

Once Cronin got his artificial foot and could walk without crutches, things got better for him. He got his old job back with the CTA. He lived up to the vow he'd made to his mother when she visited him at the Naval Hospital and he said, "Mom, I'm going to play ball again." He played park league baseball and football. He rejoined his old ice hockey team. He worked as a volunteer football coach for the boys at Angel Guardian Orphanage and at Weber High School. It was nights at the Double Bubble that Cronin would see many of his buddies who'd come home from the service and now were already on the police force.

15

One of the men who drank there, Joe Mackey, was older than Cronin but also from the neighborhood. He was a policeman on Mayor Richard J. Daley's security detail. And he'd known of Cronin's desire to become a policeman. He knew Jerry Hanrahan and Cronin had talked about going on the department together--like Jerry's dad, like Jerry's two older brothers, like half of the neighborhood. Mackey played ball with Cronin and could see what that boy could do on an artificial foot--just about anything. So one night, as he sat and talked to Cronin, he told him the written police test was coming up.

"Take it," Mackey told him. Cronin did, and he passed.

During a long limousine ride, the subject of Vietnam veterans came up between Mayor Daley and Mackey. The mayor said he was concerned about what was happening to the vets when they came home and how they were being treated by the public. The mayor wondered if they were getting the chance at jobs that they deserved. It was then that Mackey brought up Mike Cronin.

The mayor listened in the back seat and asked for Cronin's name again. He wanted to know his history and he wanted some paperwork on this kid's background. So the boy lost a foot, right? He can play ball and ice hockey and coach, right? He passed the written, right? And you say he has always wanted to be a cop?

On New Year's Eve, 1970, Mackey ran into Cronin at the 'Bubble'. Cronin seemed quiet and a bit morose. What had he heard from the department, Mackey asked? Cronin said he hadn't heard a word. Mackey tried cheering him up and then wished him Happy New Year, for he was leaving to spend the holidays guarding the mayor at his place in Michigan.

Several days later, while still in Michigan, Daley turned to Mackey and said, "What ever happened to that young fella? Did he ever get on the force?"

"You mean Mike Cronin?" said Mackey. "No, he hasn't. They never called him."

"Hmmmm," said Mayor Daley.

A week later the phone rang at the Cronin home. It was the police department. Michael J. Cronin was to report downtown for the physical exam and the agility test immediately. He took both and passed. No one, not even the examining doctor who asked him

16

to breath in deep and took a light to probe into his ears, ever asked him about his foot. On February 21, 1971, Mike Cronin walked into the Police Academy for his first class. What he thought could never be had begun.

As a thank you, Cronin sent the mayor a mass card. And said a prayer for Jerry.

THE COMMANDER NEVER SAID ANYTHING BUT I KNEW WHAT HE WAS THINKING

"The first time I went on the street I was still in the academy, and they sent us out for a month or two and then back to the academy for a short time before you got assigned to a district.

"I think it made me a little disillusioned about the police work... not discouraged, but disillusioned. I was in a slow district and one thing that will always stick out in my mind is I was supposed to be working with another guy, a field training officer, and he didn't come in so they sent me out on the street by myself. We were in the old 19th district which is now the 23rd district, and I see this guy coming down the street the wrong way. They made a mistake. They shouldn't have sent me out there by myself, but fine, out I went. And I see this guy and I stop him and he says he owns a store and he is really arrogant and doesn't care if he was going the wrong way, so what?

"He tells me, 'I know this guy, I know that guy.' I don't know anyone and didn't give a shit who he knew. I probably wouldn't have written him a ticket because I didn't know how to write a ticket if he'd said he was sorry. He didn't have a drivers license either and he was arrogant so I brought him into the station because I had to have someone help me write the ticket. He was getting increasingly arrogant, I think he said he was Greek, and he was telling me all the people he knows.

"So we get in the station and a guy I knew from growing up was the watch secretary and he sees this guy and goes over to talk to him. Then he says to me, 'You know he's a store owner and he is good to policemen.' I said, 'Well he has no license and he's a real asshole and I'm going to write him up.' He walks out of the room and I will never never forget this – this is one of the first things I remember on the job. The next thing I know the commander of the district comes out. Now I was a recruit not assigned there and he comes in and takes a look at me and walks out. He was coming in to see who I was because I was writing up some guy that was good to policemen. And that's the first thing I remember about being on the street. The commander never said anything but I knew what he was thinking–I'll get this asshole. He looked right at me and gave me a dirty look. I learned from my first arrest that there is a game you can play and I wasn't going to play that game. That's what I learned my first day. Back at the academy, the only thing I remember was learning how to drink coffee. I hated the taste but it kept me from falling asleep."

"STOLEN CAR, BROKEN GLASSES BUT HIS BIBLE WON THE CASE."

Charlie had to be at least 55. He smoked a big cigar and sometimes it seemed to get in the way of the steering wheel when it came to a demand for a sudden burst of police action --like spinning a hard right and cutting fast down an alley to answer a call. Charlie would take a few puffs and ease into the disturbance, like a grandpa in his big Buick agreeing to go out for ice cream on a Sunday night-- it was an outing not a mission. Charlie wasn't a wheel man and he didn't like moving fast. He preferred cruising to burning rubber.

When he got assigned one of those young ones, just out of the academy, itching for action, aching for an arrest, and eager to take every call that came out over the air, Charlie always made sure he drove. He grabbed the keys to the squad car after roll call. That way, he controlled where they went that night, how fast they went and when you got there. Charlie believed you didn't have to break up a fight, you just picked up the pieces.

But there was one night, back in '72, when Charlie couldn't avoid action. A clean cut black man, late in middle age and visibly frightened, ran up to Charlie's squad on the West Side and hung on the door. Oh God! They'd stolen his brand new car, he panted. He'd just pulled into the garage of his south side home, and was getting out to pull down the garage door when three male blacks rushed in on him, pulled guns, took his wallet and his coat, broke the glasses in his shirt pocket as they roughly pushed him into the trunk of the car, and drove off with him as captive. They drove around for several

21

hours, he said, and as he lay there cramped inside the trunk he could hear them talking about whether they should kill him. Should they. Shouldn't they. Should they do it now. Or wait a bit. Maybe after some fast food. The man prayed in that back trunk. Eventually, bored with their excess baggage and not in the mood at the moment to do him in, they let him out near Roosevelt Road. He emerged, trembling and confused, to find he was on the West Side. The first squad car he could find he flagged down. It was Charlie. Charlie put a flash out on the air--a call to look out for a stolen car containing three male blacks with a price tag on the rear back seat window.

The following night, Charlie got Cronin for a partner, fresh out of the academy, with the normal accoutrements of ambition and aggressiveness that drive an old timer like Charlie crazy. Cronin had been working the district the night before, but not with Charlie. He'd heard the flash come over the radio and he knew it was Charlie's voice putting it over.

Now he was with Charlie and they were heading west in the Fillmore district when a car passed them going east. It was a brand new car, had three male blacks in it and a sales sticker on the window of the rear passenger seat.

"Wasn't there a price tag on the window of that car they took last night?" Cronin asked. Charlie said, "Yeah." "Well, we just passed it, let's go after it," Cronin said. Charlie didn't say no, he just made a very awkward U-turn as if he were trying to back up and turn around an 18 wheeler on a side street. He was in no rush. Besides, his cigar got in the way of turning the wheel.

Charlie turned the wheel left, but too wide, so he then backed up, went forward, backed up again and finally went forward in hollow pursuit. As an after thought, he flicked the blue lights on.

Not two blocks down, the stolen car had made a turn and as the squad came around the corner, there it was, at a dead stop in the middle of the street, doors wide open, the inside light dimly revealing that there was nobody there. With other beat cars coming in on response, the police got out and searched the area, finding two of the men nearby, one hiding in a gangway and the other under a porch. Cronin remembered their faces and could identify them as two of the three men who passed him in the car. But he could not know if they were the armed robbers, the ones who stole the car and abducted the owner. That was up to the victim. But there was one bonus – one of the robbers was wearing the victim's jacket.

"It was my first big crime – an armed robbery. I'd never done one before," remembers Cronin. The night of the arrest, however, Charlie, didn't want his name on the report. It's not that he didn't want to take any credit, it's that he didn't want to have to go to court on this case for the next eight months. Court you did on your own time. So it was Cronin's to handle and Cronin didn't know how to type up all the forms. The man was robbed in one district, dropped off in another and flagging down a squad car in a third district. Too complicated for a rookie. The robbery detectives from the south side were called in to do the paper work. They stole the arrests, on paper, putting their names on it. But it was still an exciting case for Cronin. And he faithfully kept in touch with the victim and called him for every court date. The victim was a grandfatherly looking man, with salt and pepper hair, genteel, soft spoken and appreciative that he was not killed, that the police responded and that two of the robbers had actually been caught.

The victim was a policeman's dream. He showed up for every court appearance. He never backed down and he never gave up. And then the two offenders went on trial. The victim was there, as usual, wearing his best Sunday suit and a spit shine on well worn dress shoes when he took the stand. He was well spoken but firm in what he said.

The defense attorneys went after him in the only way they could. You made the identification of these two men, is that correct, they asked? Yes, he said, he had. And this happened in a dimly-lit garage, is that correct, they asked. Yes, he said, that is true. And they burst into that garage, pulled guns on you, roughed you up, took your money, pushed you into the trunk and in doing so broke your glasses? Yes, said the victim, that was correct.

That may very well have happened, argued the attorneys, but how could you recognize these two men as the ones who did it when your glasses were broken?

"Sir, it's true my glasses were broken," responded the victim calmly. "But, I only wear glasses when I read the Bible."

The judge glanced up. The defense threw up their hands. The prosecution smiled. In one innocent sentence the elderly gentlemen had won the case. The two offenders were sent to prison for armed robbery. The grey haired gentleman got his car back. The system had worked for him. He discreetly tried to offer Cronin $5 afterwards in the hall. For all your trouble, he said, trying to put the bill into Cronin's hand. "He thought I went out of my way for him," said Cronin. "I didn't. I only did what I was supposed to do. It was my first big caper and he was the best victim in all of my years. The lawyers didn't win that case and the police didn't win that case. That old gentleman won the case for us....with his broken glasses and a bible he believed in."

INTO THE JAWS OF DEATH

There they'd come, one driving in from the South Side, the other driving in from the North Side to meet up on the West Side. Drozd with his tiny but tidy tennis shoes. Cronin with his battered green thermos. A short but formidable duo–the "Munchkin Squad" as one detective called them because when they drove their beat up heap of a squad car you could barely see the tops of their heads.

Short little guys they were, but when they cruised through a neighborhood the lookouts spotted them and everything shut down – for a while.

"We see you and we all start running," said one street shortie, "so you don't see what we're doing."

"We know what you're doing," said Cronin, "and we see who's running and we'll be back."

"We know that, Cronin, that's why we always be looking out."

Cronin and Drozd worked the 1 p.m. to 9 p.m. shift for years as partners. Drozd would come into work with his mouth filled with wisecracks. And Cronin would come in quiet, a man unto himself.

On the street, Drozd fell silent and Cronin took over with the wise talk. Every afternoon they'd check the 24 Hour Police Report and then head out in blue jeans and flannel shirts, in parkas in the winter, with flashlights and their handcuffs and with Drozd announcing dramatically to anyone who was or was not listening to him in the Gang Crimes office: "Into the jaws of death!"

The door would close behind them and they'd be off – into one of the most violent neighborhoods in the country.

25

Many gang members got escorted to the back of their squad car where Cronin would question them and play them verbally about the action going on. "Mike will talk to them until your ears bleed," said Drozd.

They'd be out there long after 9 o'clock. Often they'd be out there after midnight. They never took a lunch break. They'd pop up sometimes at 2 in the morning, surprising the gang members who thought they knew the schedules of street policemen except for these two. It gave both of them great glee.

Their sergeant, Gene Connelly, who waited for them night after night never complained about their late hours, but did say, "My wife used to tell me she felt like she was married to a Greek with a new restaurant because I was never at home."

When the nights fell quiet and there were no adventures luring them down gangways or into abandoned houses, and the dope spots emptied out and the streets lay still, Drozd would turn to Cronin and say, "Mike, It's Miller time!" and Cronin would swing the old Chevy back toward the district and the two of them would go home. More adventure lay before them tomorrow. That they were guaranteed.

THE WEST SIDE:
THE OTHER END OF THE
YELLOW BRICK ROAD

On a clear Chicago night, you can go anywhere on Madison Street, as far west even as the city limits at Austin Avenue, and look back toward the lake and you'll see off in the distance an aura of golden light inside of which towers glow and glimmer as if encrusted with diamonds. It is a vision beckoning like the Land of Oz at the end of the yellow brick road.

It is Chicago's Loop. The Sears Tower. The Hancock Building. The AT and T Building with it's coruscating crown, and a hundred other towering monuments to money, power, commerce, success and American vitality – all clustered together like a wonderland, all golden and promising in the night and all not very far away in time or space – just a 25 minute bus ride or a 15 minute trip on the el. And yet the people on Madison Street on Chicago's West Side give it little gaze. It was as if this magic panorama to the east where the sun always rises with the promise of a new day was just an old backdrop from a previous play that has no bearing on the drama they are performing on their own stage.

Maybe they know there is no Wonderful Wizard of Oz downtown in the Loop, or perhaps they don't know that there doesn't have to be one if you just believe. Whatever the reason, the skyline that twinkles at night and gilds the clouds with gold dust is another world. And the yellow brick road that cuts straight through the West Side right up to its gates isn't heavily traveled when it comes to dreams.

Madison Street is just Madison Street, made not of yellow bricks but of potholes, old curbs and crumbling concrete. It had not always been that way but it had been falling apart from neglect for a long time.

"You had the basics out here and not much more," Cronin says, describing the West Side world he found as a new young officer. "There were seven institutions along Madison Street and that's all you got — currency exchanges, store front churches, beauty parlors, liquor stores and bars, schools, funeral parlors and fast food joints where you eat standing up."

What you didn't see along Madison Street were any banks. You'd see the emaciated skeletons of once prosperous and now long-gone banks, you'd see bank buildings that were closed and falling down, relics with the name of a bank etched in limestone over the portal. They were built to last a century but many didn't last half that. And they are all history now. People didn't use banks and they didn't open savings accounts on the West Side. They'd cash their checks at currency exchanges. Life was short, money shorter, and they'd live for today, not tomorrow. Banks were based on money tomorrow, currency exchanges on money now.

You'd see no YMCAs. They'd left this part of town and gone to the suburbs. So the boys and young men played basketball on the courts built in the projects or in school play lots. Or, like one spot on the West Side, on California Avenue, they'd play basketball on courts built by a drug dealer. The littler ones shot basketballs into a milk carton mounted on a telephone pole. Nobody much played baseball out here anymore. And you almost never saw a football being tossed around.

On Madison Street, there were no tailor shops or upholstery shops. No book stores. No new car dealerships. People on the West Side, when they wanted to buy a car would look for a cardboard sign scotch taped in the back window, purchased for $1.25, that said "For Sale By Owner" and a scribbled phone number. Good advertisement was to park it on Madison Street.

There were no music stores. No toy stores. No computer stores. No gardening stores to buy fertilizer, grass seed or a rake. No place to buy a lawnmower or a hammer or screwdriver to fix a gutter or a roof. There were no bakeries and you'd have to look real hard in the phone book to find a florist. There were no furriers, no picture framers, no paint or hardware stores. No stationery stores or card shops.

But there were endless car washes, used clothing stores, late night lounges, Arab-owned corner liquor and grocery stores, and empty lots filled with abandoned cars, old bricks, broken bottles, 10 gallon metal drums, burning tires, plastic milk crates, and sturdy wild flowers – the bluest of chicory and the whitest of Queen Anne's lace, bending ever so slightly with the winds.

This was the world Mike Cronin entered when he returned from Vietnam, healed his wounds, and realized his dream of becoming a Chicago policeman. Before that, he had only gone to the West Side for one reason in his life and that was for summer school at St. Phillips. And he hated it. He took the bus and then connected with the el and he did it for three summers. He never hated the West Side, just summer school, but when he got out of the Police Academy there was only one police district he wanted to work – Fillmore – the West Side district that crime statistics showed was the most active in the city.

The West Side has changed somewhat. But Cronin will tell you, after following three generations of street life, "not that much."

DON'T MAKE NO DIFFERENCE...
IT'S STILL THE WEST SIDE

"Look who's taking the bus, it's Dumas!"

Cronin swerved the squad car over into a bus stop at Madison and Kostner and got out.

"Dumas, my man, Dumas. Ain't seen you in a couple of years. Where you been?"

Dumas smiled.

"Laying low and minding myself. How you doing, Cronin? You still out here? Ain't you getting old for the streets?"

"You're still on them, aren't you? As long as you're around, I'll be here. They ain't getting no better."

"You got that right, Cronin," said Dumas. "Them young slicks make it hard for a man to go his own way. Man, Cronin, these ain't the same streets as when I met you. They getting fucking bad, I mean, these young boys are wild and I ain't no young boy."

Dumas was in a pink-red knit suit that fit his small and wiry body well. It was an old recycled knit suit with wide lapels, probably from a re-sale shop, but Dumas made it look dapper. He wore it with aplomb and he had on pointed loafers, white seamed silk socks that showed his dark skin underneath and sported a thin tie with a fake diamond tie clip. It looked good on him. He was wearing freshly applied cologne and his hair was short and slicked back just right, like a member of a singing group from the fifties. It was a Friday evening and Dumas was headed for action. He was just waiting for the bus to get him there.

Dumas was an old time junkie, in his late forties now. In many ways, a gentleman. He and Cronin had been young together on the streets when they met. He'd been ducking and dealing with Cronin since he put the first needle into his vein.

"You look good, Dumas, what are you doing, taking vitamins?" asked Cronin.

"Nah, Cronin, just slowing down. I got married, you know, and I got a place to lay low. I'm not playing the way I was."

"You want to get into the car for a minute?" asked Cronin

"Sure, Cronin, but I'm waiting for the bus."

"If you miss the bus I'll take you there," said Cronin.

"I don't want you knowing where I'm going," said Dumas, laughing.

"Then I'll flag it down, okay? Get in. We can't talk out here."

Dumas climbed in back, rolled down the window, knowing from habit Cronin's aversion to cigarette smoke, and lit up a Kool.

"Man, I been here before," he said, looking around the back of the unmarked squad.

"You got any warrants on you, Dumas?" asked Cronin.

"Shit Cronin! You know I don't. I'm clean."

"You still doing brown, is there any around?" asked Cronin.

"The action ain't the same. There ain't no brown (heroin) out here. The young ones be doing white and they all crazy. Remember Cronin, when you used to hit the dope strolls? There were a couple good ones on the West Side and you were always riding on us but they was safe. Now they be selling drugs from every step and corner and they kill you for it. These young slicks are crazy, Cronin. I take a hit every once in a while, but I be slowing down. I drink a little wine now instead."

"Dumas, you ARE slowing down. You're right, those young boys are wild. They are sixteen years old and they'd kill someone like you in a minute if they could get something off you. They wouldn't look back at you bleeding."

Dumas shook his head in agreement and straightened his lapels, anxious to hop out and not miss the bus. He re-adjusted a political pin that said "EVANS FOR MAYOR" on it. He re-pinned it so that it was prominent on his suit.

"You going to vote in the next election," Cronin asked, watching him.

"Shit, no!" said Dumas, with an 'are-you-kidding' chuckle.

"What do you mean, you're wearing a campaign pin?"

"This button don't mean nothing," said Dumas. "You know what this is?" and he pointed to the button. "I call this West Side jewelry. You know, someone was handing it out for free and you put it on and walk four blocks and if it don't match your suit you throw it away. I got nothing to do with voting. I ain't even registered."

"Why not, Dumas?" asked Cronin. "Evans is black. You could help elect another black mayor--like Harold."

"Cause, Cronie," said Dumas leaning forward toward the front seat and throwing his cigarette out the back window, earnest now and no longer bullshitting. "Cause it don't make no difference. You know, Cronie. You been here. The West Side was the West Side under Daley. The West Side was the West Side under Byrne. The West Side was the West Side under Harold Washington. Don't matter who's down at City Hall, black or white, they all forget this place. The West Side going to be the West Side, no matter who's down there. That's the way it is and that's the way it's going to stay. OOOOOOP...later, Cronie," said Dumas suddenly and he hopped out of the car.

His bus had come. And it WAS Friday night.

"YOU SHOULD HAVE SEEN ME, CRONIE. I WAS GOOD ONCE."

There was Rat, loping down Madison street with a wide easy gait, totally involved in fried chicken. He wasn't looking up, or around or behind, like he normally would do. He was too hungry. He had a cardboard food container up three inches from his mouth like a trough and his eyes were on the cole slaw and fried chicken that his fingers were shoveling into his mouth. Forget the plastic fork.

Rat was eating the way he's lived his life-- on the run. But Rat wasn't up for running tonight. Just easy loping and letting the food slide down as he was passing the bar-b-que and chicken joints, their neon signs blinking with half the letters burnt out, passing the open doors of saloons where the smell of stale beer was still sticking to the floor.

Passing the guys on the corner, and he knew them all, passing through the sweet smell of reefer left by someone who'd exhaled and moved on. Passing the old timers leaning against the windows of an out-of-business store front church, enjoying a Kool they begged from a smart looking fox with red nails and a cigarette laugh. Passing the young slicks in hooded sweatshirts who nodded and let him pass unhassled because they'd heard that Rat was good once.

"Straight up, it's true man, he was better than his brother Isaiah."

Better than anyone on the West Side has ever been. Could have been better than anyone in the country. Could've. Could've been a millionaire. Could've been a celebrity. Could've been on TV and owned a ranch house you'd see in Ebony magazine. Could've escaped off Madison street. But the fast life had grabbed onto his ankles and hadn't let go. So partly in respect for what he could've been and partly because of who Rat's brother was, Rat loped unmolested down the sidewalk, a 'could've been' that nobody bothered anymore.

This night, Rat was not worrying about nothing, including the police and that wasn't like Rat. For Rat was a man with pepper in his shoes. The very sight of a police car would have him hot-footing over a fence, down a gangway and out of sight. He was no longer the athlete he once was but he could still ditch his own shadow.

He hadn't eaten in over 24 hours. He was tired and his chest hurt. It had been hurting a lot lately. With a little food going down, he was starting to feel good. And he'd feel even better in a little while. So he kept loping easy, his eyes on his food, his guard down and then....

"Rat!"

And there was Mike Cronin climbing out of the squad car just five feet in front of him. Cronin, getting out fast, without closing the driver's door, heading right for him, and yelling like he always does: "Rat!"

"Cronin!" said Rat, looking up, a look of ambush in his eyes. Was there a warrant out on him? Must be or Cronin wouldn't be yelling. Rat dropped his chicken plate flat on the street and took off. Cronin took off after him, the two running down the street, but the police officer fell quickly behind. Rat was around the corner and gone. Cronin was still shouting before the turn.

"What was that?"said a woman whose arms were filled with groceries who had turned to watch.

"That's just Rat and Cronin," chuckled an older man. "They do that all the time."

For years, Rat has been running from Cronin. And from every other cop. And from his family. From the talent he once had as a youth. From opportunity. From reform. From the memory of what he "could've been." He wasn't just running away from Cronin. Rat was running away from everything. Cronin couldn't outrun Rat, but he could catch him.

"Why do you always run on me, Rat?" Cronin would ask him one night, after many a pursuit, when he finally did.

"Cause, Cronie. You catch me at the wrongest places," Rat would say with a smile.

"You ain't that fast anymore," Cronin would say.

"I can still run, Cronin," Rat would answer.

"Fuck, if I had two feet you wouldn't beat me," Cronin would say, and they would stare at each other across the back of the driver's seat for a half a second and laugh. And then Cronin would get on the police radio and check for a warrant. There was often one out on Rat who continually failed to show up in court on one petty theft charge or another.

If there was, Cronin would handcuff Rat's hands to the back of his seat because Rat had a habit of jumping out of the squad if he and the car were not inextricably connected. He did it once with handcuffs on.

Remember, Cronin, when I jumped out on you with my handcuffs on and ran through the mall...there was a warrant out on me that night."

"I remember," said Cronin. "We spotted you in the back of the mall at Homan and Jackson and put you in the back seat of the car, handcuffed."

"And I jumped out the rear door and ran through the mall and Kenny Smooth was sitting at Homan a few blocks down on his motorcycle and you were chasing me and he saw me coming and he started it up and I jumped on behind him with the handcuffs behind my back and he gunned it and I fell off 'cause I was too tired from running ... and I couldn't hold on..."

"Plus, you tripped before you even got on and then you fell off..."

"And you caught me, Cronin."

"Yeah, we caught you, Rat. You got to have more than fast feet to get away."

But on this evening in May, Rat got away. He'd lost the chicken dinner he was savoring and went to bed hungry. His chest was probably hurting worse from the running. But he escaped.

Running was a game for Rat. The only game left for him to play for he'd dropped out of all the others. When it came to crime, Rat didn't play the big leagues. He never was wanted for anything other than petty crimes--mostly thievery. Cronin never knew Rat to carry a gun. He'd arrested him three or four times on a warrant--for Rat ran from his court appearances too--but he'd never caught Rat with any drugs. Rat wasn't a seller, he was a user.

"Rat is the kind that once he gets his dope, he lays up for a while," says Cronin. "You don't catch him with it. Problem is, Rat's been using too long. Rat has been able to outrun everything except the streets he's running on."

It is drugs--first marijuana, then pills, then heroin-- that made Rat a "could've been." Everyone on the street who's pushing forty has told Cronin he should have seen Rat when he was 16. Rat was the best there was on the court, better than his now famous baby brother. His brother made it big time. So could've Rat--once.

"You should have seen me Cronin, I was good," Rat has confessed to Cronin, but not to many others.

Rat is no student of history but he knows his name never got entered in the book. Not that history wasn't waiting for him.

"I was 5'11" and you couldn't touch me back then. I'm talking about seven footers. They couldn't touch me. I was great at the game. All I dreamed of was the NBA."

"And the first time you went and got a bag of dope and put it in your arm, you were through," Cronin said. "And so was your dream of the NBA."

"I know it could've been me. What my brother is I could've been. But I fucked up, Cronin. And it hurts. I'm hurting now. But I can't leave what I've become."

"You got it in your blood, Rat," Cronin said.

"I know, Cronin," Rat said back. "I'd jump over 100 buildings to figure out how to get it out of me. I'm over forty and I don't have nothing. I don't own a house. I don't have a job. I don't have a wife. I got the streets, that's all. I got nothing but the streets."

It was on the streets that Cronin again met Rat, two months after Rat had dropped his chicken dinner and beat it around the corner. This time Cronin spotted him in the back seat of a Mercedes-Benz being driven by Baby Ty, a well known drug dealer, and the car had just slid up to a curb on Homan Avenue. The passengers were all about to pile out, in fact the curbside door opened when they were greeted with :

"Rat!" Cronin said like he always does. He was waiting on the sidewalk for him.

"Cronin!" Rat said, like he always says, looking ambushed like he always does and ready to run like he always is. But there was no place to run.

They both climbed into the squad car and drove down the street. Rat was wearing a Bulls sweat shirt and, it being a hot night, he was sweating profusely. But he smiled a lot and spoke in a somewhat soft, if not resigned voice. Many of his teeth were missing. Rat looked beat up by the fast life.

"You know, I'm getting too old to be doing this. My body, my heart. You know, I can't take it," Rat said.

"I got you Rat," said Cronin, chuckling. "For two years, every time I pull up you run on me."

"Cronin, I been running on you all my life," said Rat, who laughed and his laugh was like a whinny, nasal and through his nose, like a wild stallion with a sense of humor.

"No, just for twenty years, since I got on the job," said Cronin.

"I want to talk to you. Where do you want to talk?"

"Just pull up over here," said Rat. They pulled over somewhere dark and Cronin cut the motor of the car. It was July 3rd and far away, way up in the sky to the east, you could see the city fire works exploding in tiny golden bursts over the highest sky line in the world.

Downtown was so far away, and yet so near, that you could see the rockets' eruptions only as Tinker-Bell dust falling to the ground. You could not even hear a muffled pop when they burst and spread their glistening spores – like pennies aglitter – out into the night sky. But none of them landed on the West Side.

"Is there a warrant out for you, Rat?"

"Cronin, you know I'm just a little old petty thief and I don't do nothing in your area."

"How's your health, you son of a bitch. You don't look so good."

"Not good, Cronin. I got chest pains. I should be in the hospital because I'm having these pains."

"Why'd you run on me, Rat?"

"Cause that's what I always do."

39

"Bullshit. A lot of water has run under the bridge. Do you think if I really wanted you and I spent time looking, I couldn't catch you?"

"I know you could, Cronin. Am I going to get locked up tonight?"

"Is there a warrant out on you? Do you think I want to spend the time chasing you for some bullshit warrant knowing you'll be right back out. Last summer you were selling dummy dope on Madison and Parkside. You're lucky you didn't get killed."

"Am I going to get locked up?"

"I don't know. Is there a warrant out? There always is because you have a bad habit of not showing up in court."

"I forget," said Rat, whinnying.

"Rat," said Cronin, "are people bullshitting me when they say you were better than your brother? A lot of people have said it. What age were you? 15? 16?"

"I was good," Rat said.

"You know, I heard your brother say it on TV," said Cronin. "What the shit happened to you, Rat? Your brother made it and you didn't and you were better."

"I ran into a hot woman, Cronin. It was my junior year in high school and she introduced me to dope. In this neighborhood, in the sixties, is when drugs caught on and it caught on with me. Right there, at the old Hoover Hotel, that's where I bought dope. I was at St. Phillips, cause I'd been going to Catholic schools all my life, and she was at Marshall. They were going to kick me off the basketball team because I had too many absences but they gave me make up tests and I passed all the make up tests but the teachers all had to agree to let me stay and one teacher, the English teacher, wouldn't agree to it and I got kicked off the team and out of school. So then, cause I could play basketball, I went to Hales and Farragut and DePaul and Marshall and more than that..."

"Why did you do that, Rat, if you were dreaming about playing basketball?"

"Cause I was using dope and I guess I was trying to find myself."

"Did you ever graduate?"

"I graduated in the Army. I got drafted. I got my GED in the Army in 1969 and then the Army kicked me out.

"Why were you playing so stupid?"

"Cronin, I'm telling you the truth. It might sound naive to you but I was a sheltered child. We had to be in the house as soon as it got dark. I was snorting dope for two years and didn't know it was the same thing people were putting in their arms...

"Cut the shit, Rat."

"It's the truth, Cronin. But by then, I liked it. I got kicked out of high school, got kicked out of the Army. I played basketball for Wright and for DePaul...."

"You went to college? You played for them?" asked Cronin incredulously.

"For a minute," said Rat. "Then I just stopped going. By that time the streets had got a hold of me."

"The streets and dope," said Cronin.

"The streets is what's in dope, Cronin," said Rat. "I'm just saying, being in the fast life. Okay. Like saying there's a dope dealer that don't even use drugs but the idea... it's not even the money that they are there for – it's being in the fast life. Being around fast women and all that, that's more addictive than the drugs. Drugs, I could have quit the drugs. This is more than likely why I haven't. I could quit drugs but I'd be bored to death. If I quit drugs, I'd have to turn square. Live a normal life and I'd be bored."

"Would it be boring living the life of a basketball star like your brother?"

"To me it would. I'd rather be around whores and dope dealers."

"I believe that, Rat," said Cronin. "Your brother would take you anytime wouldn't he? He bails you out of jail all the time. He'd take you anytime if you'd straighten out."

"Oh yeah," said Rat. "If I wanted a house built, he would build it for me. But I wouldn't be content. Not now. Not me now. I don't think I could learn different. I'd rather be around the fast life. I know I've done wrong. I know I'm dumb. I'm stupid for doing the shit that I do because I don't have to do it but I continue to do it. It's hard to explain.

"I wish I never ran into that English teacher that got me kicked out of high school. I don't blame it all on him. I blame it on me because I wasn't strong enough. Like my parents, they were good parents, but

41

they weren't street wise. All my brothers played basketball except Gay Gay and he became a junkie too. And all of them could have played professional basketball. It took five brothers to hold my baby brother back and say to him, 'You are going to be the one.' It took five brothers to sit out to dry and say, 'It's you. We're not going to let you go. You are the one who is going to make it.'"

"How did you keep the street away from him?" asked Cronin.

"Wouldn't let anyone near him. All that kid did everyday was go to school, play basketball and come home. We protected him."

"You know, I've heard about your mother," said Cronin, "but I never heard about your father."

"My father is dead. Died a couple of years ago. He's the one who knocked my teeth out," said Rat. "He was a machinist. You know, if my mom went to the store and came back, she got to show the receipt.

"If it was a penny short, he would want to beat her up and stuff. We always fought when I was little about my mom. I was the oldest. Then he jumped on my mom on Mothers Day. I was old enough to think I could beat him. Everybody had on new clothes except me and I was going to get some money for new clothes 'cept he came home and beat my mom up on Mothers Day and took the money for my new clothes to go gambling and I went down there to the hotel where he was gambling the money and there was a restaurant in there called the Golden Eagle and him and me got to fighting. I was seventeen. I come back home and went to bed. I weighed 128 pounds and my dad was 6'2" and over 200 pounds and he came home later, caught me in bed sleeping and beat my ass. I woke up in the hospital beat up and my teeth knocked out. My dad left home by the time my baby brother was coming up."

"Rat," said Cronin. "I got to find out if this is a true story. Some say that you went to Detroit in a limousine on 'Say No to Drugs Day' and bought dope and scared the shit out of the white limousine driver, your brother's driver."

"Yeah," said Rat. "My brother got a limousine he rents all the time. Who told you that? Shit, you know everything Cronin. Yeah, it was two years ago and the first Say No to Drugs Day Detroit ever had. My brother was the head of it.

"He started it. He was the speaker. So me and my other brother, Gay Gay, he use drugs too, we go up there and we are all in tuxedos and we are guests at the Mayor's Ball. After a few minutes, Gay Gay wants to go and get some dope, even though the dope dealers said they'd lay off from selling for one night. But Gay Gay says, 'Let's get out of here and get some dope.' The limousine was waiting outside. We in tuxedos and all that shit so we go out to this white limousine driver and we don't ask him about drugs, cause that ain't cool on this day. We ask him where the prostitutes hang out and he said something like 10th street, so we said to take us where the whores are. So he takes us there and through the window we ask the whores where the drugs is. But they are scared cause we are in a limousine with a white driver so Gay Gay and I got out of the car and showed them our arms so they wouldn't think we were the police. 'We're just from out of town,' we told them, 'from Chicago'. The white driver was scared to death."

"I heard the driver told your brother he won't do that any more," said Cronin.

"It WAS the day everyone agreed to stop selling drugs...but how you know what the driver told my brother?"

"I heard about it on the street, Rat. So you...and you were the oldest , right?"

"Right, then come Gay Gay."

"So you and Gay Gay, the two oldest got into drugs?"

"No," said Rat. "The three oldest boys. Larry too, but he clean now. He's got a talk show in Detroit about drugs."

"Well, which one is the policeman," asked Cronin.

"There were eight of us, six boys and two sisters" said Rat. "One of my brothers who come after the first three is the policeman."

"So Rat, what happened in this family? You got your brother in Detroit. He is a hero. Kids idolize him. He does a lot of good and public service. He is a millionaire athlete. Then you got a brother who's a cop. Good middle class brother with a middle class job. Then here you are, selling dummy dope, thieving and running from me. A junkie. It's like you all come from different worlds but you come from the same family. Your baby brother lives like a king--and yeah, he earned it. He's at one end, the rich end. Then you got your brother, the policeman, he's in the middle..and at the bottom end... there's a brother living in the fucking ghetto and a drug addict."

"I'm the drug addict. I'm at the bottom. I know. But my mama don't know...," said Rat.

"She don't know what?" asked Cronin.

"She don't know what I do."

"What does she think you do?" asked Cronin.

"I think I worry her to death wondering," said Rat.

"I saw on TV a movie about your brother and it showed how the gang members came to your house, to your mama's house, and tried to get your baby brother into a gang and she pulled a shot gun and chased them off. But they weren't there for your brother at all. They were there for you, right?"

"Yeah, I ran off with some dope. They were there looking for me. They wanted me. They just wanted their money back and I was hiding. They didn't want my brother...but my mama don't know that. It looked good on TV."

"Your brother has a summer camp," said Cronin. "Wouldn't you like to go work with kids at a summer camp? Look. You could do more to fight drugs than your brother ever hoped to. Do you know that?"

"Yeah," said Rat. "I know."

"With his name and what you've been through, if you would straighten up. Your brother can't tell the kids what drugs are all about. I can't tell kids what drugs are all about. Fuck, you've witnessed it. You've lived it. You could do more than your brother. Kids will listen to your brother saying don't do it. But you can tell them why not to do it, from your own personal experiences. With his name attached, they'll listen to you."

"You know, I'd love that. Cronin."

"Love that, my ass. You could do it, Rat," said Cronin. "It might be a little demeaning and downgrading for you to tell them how the fuck you lived for the last 30 years but you could help a lot of fucking kids. You could help yourself too. Your brother is on the outside looking in. You Rat, are on the inside looking out. Does your brother ever talk to you about this?"

"You got to realize, he my baby brother..."

"I think he's kinda given up on you," said Cronin. "Sure, he'll bond you out and shit, but as much as he's tried to help you..."

"He can't do nothing more money wise," said Rat, "cause money won't help me. I got to help me. All he tells me is, 'Whenever you are ready, let me know'."

"And what does that mean?"

"It mean what it takes to get me back in society and start a new life..."

"And when will that be, Rat? Shit, it ain't going to happen."

"Hopefully, very soon. My body says I'm ready but I still like doing dope. Don't you know I would love to get up and go to work from 9 to 5 and come home and be able to rest. JUST BE ABLE TO REST. And not get up every fucking morning with a monkey on my back. Cronin, I'm so fucking tired."

"The street has fucking changed since you started doing dope, hasn't it Rat? You are a seasoned veteran...an old timer...and lucky to still be alive."

"The game has changed, Cronin," said Rat. "The whole code and ethics of dope has changed. Twenty years ago you couldn't buy from somebody you didn't know. When I was growing up, you might find ten dope fiends in one neighborhood and it was all done secretly. They didn't come out on a corner and advertise it like this is the way of the world. Back then, a dope dealer didn't sell no dope to kids. When I started, I had to get an older guy to buy it for me. Now, it's kids selling it. Kids running it. Kids using it.

"The whole world is strung out. Not just here in Chicago on the West Side. The whole world, as I know it. I ain't never seen so many dope fiends...I see a lost generation coming, Cronin. My kids, and I got four kids by two different women, my kids are lost. I mean that as far as black children. Like I come up on the streets. I don't have time to raise my kids so therefore they raise themselves. They and the other kids with them, they going to be dope dealers and dope users. It's going to get worse. There's already a hundred people waiting to make a buy on some of these corners. We're looking at thirty to forty years of lost people."

"So you know that, Rat, what else do you know?" said Cronin. "Talk to me. Tell me something good, name some spots where there's guns and dope."

45

Rat mumbles some spots he knows.

Are they bagging it there or selling from there? Is it the third apartment to the right, white porch up on the third floor? Does it have a security gate? Is someone living there or is it a bag house? Do they keep guns there? Are they wearing the guns or are they hidden? Under the floor? Behind a cushion of the couch? Is it a 24 hour operation? How many lookouts? Cronin was talking about raiding the place.

"Cronin, when you do it and get the dope, I want some," said Rat, grinning.

"Rat, the last time I looked, I wasn't a fucking drug dealer," said Cronin.

"In New York, don't they do it that way?"

"Hey," said Cronin, getting testy. "In Paris they wear a certain uniform but I don't dress the way they do in Paris. And I don't do things like they do in New York. They ain't anybody out here ever say I gave them dope. And you ain't getting zippo."

"I know that, Cronin. God damn. I was just saying something to fill the air."

"Spare the air. It's filled with enough Bullshit out here. You know, someday you are going to run on me and have a heart attack and I'm going to have to get back in the car and leave you," said Cronin, still mad.

"Would you do that to me?" asked Rat, truly curious.

"What am I supposed to do? You ran, not me. What am I supposed to do, give you mouth to mouth?"

"I'd give you mouth to mouth, Cronin," said Rat.

"The fuck you would. That would really kill me. I'd die after that."

The two laughed together. Cronin started the car, which was parked under the shadows of foliage on a dead-end street near the expressway. You could hear the trucks passing without seeing them and the leaves that spilled on top of the discreetly parked squad car were covered with highway soot. They hadn't been green since May and needed to be dusted. As Cronin put the car in drive, the squad lumped forward, listed to the right, and lumped forward again.

"We got a fucking flat, I know it," said Cronin banging out of the car and swearing when he looked at a suffocated rear tire.

"I'll help you, Cronin. Can I get out?" said Rat, leaning his head out the back window.

"Might as well, Rat. You going to run on me again?"

"No," said Rat. "I'm going to help you."

"You just hold this there and I'll get this..." and the two bent over together, like men do, grunting and bending when they jack up a car, then pulling out the spare from the trunk, bouncing it over to the spot where the other tire had withered and dusting off their hands once it was there and in place.

The chaser and the chasee. They might not meet again in years. But this night, they changed a tire together, like old friends who for a few minutes forgot they were on different sides of the law and always would be.

They climbed back into the car, Cronin behind the wheel, Rat in the back seat, right behind Cronin.

Cronin started the car and it no longer limped along the curb. It was ready to roll.

"You aren't going to lock me up tonight, are you?" asked Rat.

"No Rat, I'm not, because I never called in to name check you. You aren't wanted on a warrant are you? I'll take your word. But I don't know why I'm doing this after all the shit you give me. If I ever see you again and you run on me...."

"You'll see me going around a corner sometime, somewhere, Cronin," said Rat.

"If you run on me, we got nothing else to say to each other anymore," said Cronin.

"Okay," said Rat. "We got an understanding."

Cronin pulled onto the Eisenhower Expressway.

"You are going to let me go, right? Are you taking me out west?" asked Rat.

"Oh. I'm supposed to take you out west? I don't see a meter in this fucking car. I don't believe you are asking..."

"I was just assuming that you would, Cronin," said Rat.

"After all the times I had to chase you?"

"Cronie?"

"Rat!"

"Cronie. Please. I'm not feeling so good. Look at me."

"I've looked at you twice, Rat. Three strikes and you're out."

"Drop me off out west, in Austin, Cronin."

At four in the morning, Cronin dropped Rat off. It was in the middle of a side street and there was no one afoot. No headlights in the distance. Several blocks down the stop lights switched from red to green but there were no cars there to obey. It commanded nobody but the dark and blinked only to the night. The city had expended itself on a holiday eve and it now was asleep. No one was looking. So Rat didn't have to run.

"You better be careful then, especially in this weather," Cronin said, almost tenderly. He handed him a few bucks and said, "You got a place to sleep?"

"Sure, Cronin. I got lots of places to sleep," said Rat. "Sure. I can go to my mama's. I got friends. I can call my brother..I even got a girl friend who stay near by."

Rat stepped out of the car. He didn't run when he got out. His chest hurt and he was sweating despite the pre-dawn chill. He needed to be alone. He walked a hundred paces down the middle of the street and then turned suddenly and ducked into an alley. In the distance, the stoplight went from green to red and as far as Cronin could see, the ribbon of pavement was hollow-- without a reflection of movement or life.

Once again, Rat was gone. The 'could've been' had disappeared. There was no sign of him, not even a fleeting shadow. The streets have short memories.

POST SCRIPT: Cronin didn't see Rat again, that year or for several years. Rat seemed to have truly vanished. Then one evening toward the end of the summer of 1997 Cronin stopped to talk to a group of old junkies chilling out against a wall at

Madison and Francisco. Just street talk. Who knew what and who claimed to know nothing. Cronin knew most of them by name and those he didn't, knew him. Afterwards he pulled a half a block up in the squad car to sit and watch the corner. A man came up to his car and leaned into the passenger side window.

"Cronin!" said the man, toting a big grin.

"Yeah, man," said Cronin. It was no one he knew.

"You don't recognize me, do ya?"

"No, my man, I don't."

"Rat."

"Rat?" Cronin looked more closely.

"I'm straight, Cronin."

"Shit you look good...where you been? I've been looking for you."

"Left town and went straight a couple of years ago."

Rat was thirty pounds heavier and he was dressed well, in a pastel short sleeved shirt. The once raw track marks on his arms had dried into quiet scars. He wasn't sweating. He'd made it, he told Cronin.

"That's good. You beat the streets, Rat."

"I owe some of it to you, Cronin."

"For what, Rat? For all the times I chased you, you son of a bitch?"

"No, Cronin, for all the times you caught me."

"Cronin ain't big but he scares them. He ain't as fast as them but he catches them. They act like they own the streets but day after day Cronin goes out there and reminds them the streets aren't theirs to own. They think they're tough, heroic fighters but they've never been through what Cronie's big through. He's so straight he intimidates them."

– A West Side police officer

SMASH DOWN THE DOOR ...
WE'RE HAVING A BABY

They saw the man before he saw them. He was acting funny, looking right, looking left, waiting outside a basement door on Ohio Street, but not going in. Like he didn't have a key and it wasn't his place, but there was something inside he wanted.

Cronin and Drozd bumped the Blue Dragon – their old squad car – up over the curb and across the empty lot that was adjacent to the building and stopped 15 feet from the basement side door.

The man saw them when they were half way up to him, two short white guys in jeans, tennis shoes, parkas, long black flashlights tucked in their belts...no, tucked into handcuffs hanging off their belts. Flashlights. Handcuffs. Not a good sign.

He walked away, causally. Just kept walking until he disappeared round the alley. The two policemen didn't try to stop him. They went down three stairs to the basement door, looked around in a curious manner, poked a flashlight through the metal accordion gates and knocked on the inside door.

After a few seconds, two small, tightly wrapped tin foil packets were squeezed out under the door. Drozd reached down, picked them up and unwrapped them. It was heroin.

"Shit, he thinks we're the guy that just left, Mike. He was waiting for his two bags of heroin and we chased him away."

"They are fucking dealing down here," said Cronin, starting to pound, with the butt of his flashlight, through gaps in the security gate onto the inside door.

"Yo!" he said. But there was no answer.

"Open up! You got fucking dope in there, asshole," said Cronin. "It's the police."

There was not an audible stir inside. They tried pulling the accordion door open but it was padlocked. They couldn't budge it.

"You get a fucking warrant, I ain't opening up," said a male voice from inside. Cronin and Drozd kept kicking the gate and banging on the door, furious now as the voice inside kept badgering them with, "I ain't opening up."

"We got you. We got your damn dope, you gave it to us," yelled Cronin. "We got you fucking cold."

"Get a warrant," taunted the voice from inside.

Through the kicking and banging and their incessant rattling of the security gate they heard a scream, and then another, coming from inside. They stopped to listen. And then moans. It sounded like a woman.

The "Get a warrant"routine had stopped. There was silence. The male voice on the inside of the door had quieted in response to the screams behind him. The two policemen tried to listen but it was hard to hear anything when the bars of the security gate stopped them from laying an ear next to the door.

All of a sudden, someone was pounding on the door, this time from the inside. It was frantic and the same voice that told them defiantly to get a warrant was now begging them to bash the door down and come in.

"You've got to help me," the male voice said. "Kick in the door. I don't know what to do. She's having a baby."

"A what?" said Drozd.

"A baby. My girlfriend's having a baby right now. Right down here and I can't get out."

"Open the goddamn door, then," said Cronin.

"I cain't," said the male voice. "It's locked for the night. For my shift. They give us some drugs to sell, lock us in, take the key and don't come back for eight hours. Now, she having a baby and I cain't get out an she need help. You got to smash in the door. We're having a baby. Please..."

The man was almost crying.

"When's the motherfucker with the key due back?" asked Cronin.

"Not for five more hours...please officer! If he sees you he won't come at all."

Cronin and Drozd looked at each other.

"How old are you?" yelled Cronin through the door.

"Sixteen," came the answer.

"How old is the girl?"

"Seventeen. This is her third baby and she need help. Kick down the door officer."

"We've been trying," said Cronin. "They're juveniles. And their baby's being born in a dope den," he mumbled. "That's great. Great future for all of them."

Drozd got on the radio. He called for paramedics. But the paramedics could do nothing if they couldn't get in. So he called for backup from Gang Crimes and told them to bring forced entry tools-sledge hammers and the Chicago bar. They were going to have to rip both doors down to get in. Within fifteen minutes they did.

The boy was still pounding on the door from the inside when it came down. On a grimy, naked mattress, they found the girl, legs folded up clutching her large belly heaving with the birth effort. The paramedics carefully put her on a gurney and carried her away shortly afterwards. The sixteen year old father was not at her side. He was taken to the station where he admitted that he had been selling from that damp and windowless basement room for three weeks. He was charged as a juvenile for selling heroin and turned over to youth officers.

Having Drozd and Cronin pounding at the basement door that night was a rare chance at luck for this hapless couple. Getting them to tear the door down spared the new baby's life, perhaps, but it did not change the future of things for all three of them.

"They are prisoners of drugs," said Cronin later, after it was all over. "And pulling them out of that dope spot tonight doesn't mean they aren't still trapped. We ripped off the security gate and we knocked down the door. But believe me, they are all still prisoners. The police did not make them free. Remember, we never found the key."

JERRY DID HIS BEEF IN THE CHAIR

On many a warm summer night, and even when there is a slight chill, Jerry will sit on the corner with Blue and listen to the night sounds. They become less blurred and more distinct once twilight fades and dark descends. Jerry cocks an ear and listens. He knows those night sounds well. He once was a player of the night. His youthful adrenalin pumped with the nightly call to action-- the ripping and running of a young man, strong, defiant, unencumbered by fear or hindered by rules. He could catch the distinct tenor of male voices down on the corner challenging each other on a Friday night. He recognized the degree of urgency in the rhythm of footsteps through a gangway. He was instinctively alert to the bumpity- bump beat of a banged up police squad pulling into the alley. He could tell the caliber of the gun when shots were fired two blocks away...their sharp crackle measuring from major to minor. The night and its sounds used to send him into motion, as if the West Side after dusk was an orchestra and he the dancer who knew all the steps.

Although the music continues, louder and stronger than ever each night, Jerry can now only listen. He can't dance to the tune anymore. Not because, at 39, he is too old for the streets. But because from the waist down, he is paralyzed from a bullet that burrowed into his spine.

But he still can listen each summer night to the West Side's calamitous symphony. He does it from his wheel chair with his sidekick Blue. He knows what the music is saying. He's just not a part of it anymore. The new dance troupe has forgotten him.

Cronin remembered this old time dancer. And he stopped his squad car when he saw him on the corner. He remembered that Jerry was sticking up a gas station at Taylor and Sacramento when he got shot back in 1972. He remembered that during the holdup Jerry shot and killed a man working there. He remembers that Jerry went to the joint for what he did.

"What are you doing out here, my man?" asked Cronin.

"Just talking to the fellahs," said Jerry. "Hell, nothing else to do."

"Funny, I don't see no fellahs around," said Cronin. "And you – what's your name?" Cronin said turning to the sidekick.

"My name Blue, you remember me Cronin," said Blue. "You got me over there couple of years ago on armed robbery."

"You ain't sitting on no guns, are you Jerry?" asked Cronin.

"I don't carry no gun, Cronie. I'm not allowed to carry no gun," said Jerry.

"That's right. You been to the joint."

"I did ten and a half years, Cronin. For murder," said Jerry. "I got twenty to sixty but I did ten and a half years. And I did the beef in this chair."

"You killed a guy during a stick-up right? I remember," said Cronin.

"Now this is actually what happened. I could never prove it. And I could still sue for this but...they twisted it around Cronin. I wasn't doing no hold up. They said I stuck up a gas station and killed the guy and got shot doing it. But I got stuck up and robbed for $8.50. and shot besides. They twisted it around on me, Cronin. And I had to do that beef in this chair."

"Are you a Black Soul?" Cronin asked, trying to recall.

"Am I a Black Soul? I founded the Black Souls."

"My man, were you a Black Soul when you were in the joint?"

"I started the Black Souls. Me and Pee Wee. Pee Wee got killed right behind me. Matter of fact, it wasn't even a week after I got shot he died. There was a hit out on us back then and I was trying to get out of town when I got shot."

"Yeah, you were trying to get enough money to leave town," said Cronin.

Jerry chuckled and made no reply.

"So if you are an old time chief, and the founder of the Black Souls. Did you go to Big C's birthday party he threw for himself last week on the south side?" asked Cronin. "He's a big time Black Soul now."

"I did," said Blue .

"I didn't," said Jerry quietly. "I was home in bed watching HBO. But I got the scoop. I heard they were serving Dom Perignon."

"They were serving ribs, meatballs, chicken wings and shit," said Blue. "You had to bring the Dom Perignon for the birthday boy, not for you."

"Yeah, and everybody on the invitation list was a dope dealer," said Cronin. "The girls were users. The men were sellers and those not selling were using. This was a dope dealers' party. Not like the old days, right Jerry, when gangs didn't mix. Now gangs mix because dope is dope, right?"

"I hear you," said Jerry. "And dope don't have no gang colors."

"That's right," said Cronin, "cause money is all green."

Jerry stopped for a minute and turned his head toward some sounds coming from the alley.

"So, why you out here now? You're an old man for this stuff," said Cronin.

"I sit here and listen, Cronin, that's all I can do now," said Jerry."Don't play no more."

"He like a celebrity to us when they stop," said Blue.

"Oh? And who stops? Who gives a penny to him when they drive by? Who even knows his name anymore," said Cronin.

"See," said Blue, "he like a little celebrity to them now I guess cause he is paralyzed and when they see him they stop and give him a holler."

"A holler my ass," said Cronin. "There's nobody stopping here. The young players aren't anywhere around and they don't care. Celebrity? The streets don't remember celebrities any longer than tomorrow. You know, my man. You may remember being a chief of the Black Souls but these home boys were in diapers back then and the young Black Souls don't remember you. You're riding in a wheel chair and they are riding past you in Cadillacs. They ain't giving you no holler. They ain't giving you shit."

"I hear ya, Cronin," said Jerry, looking not at the policeman but wistfully down the street. "I hear ya straight."

"Blue?" he said, turning to his faithful sidekick. But Blue's hands were already on the handles of his wheelchair and his foot was kicking off the brake. "Blue," he said. "Let's try another corner before it get too cold and too late."

THE GIRL WITH A HOLE IN HER HEART

It was a cheap little purse--pink plastic meant to look like patent leather. A small clutch bag a girl child carries when she is playing dress up. Hers was all beat up-- with cracks in the plastic and it didn't snap shut when you tried to close it. She'd probably had it a long time.

There wasn't much inside. A natty comb, chewing gum, some loose pennies, two barrettes, some gold eye shadow and a piece of lined tablet paper folded up and worn at the seams like a frayed shirt collar. The ordinary was missing. No keys. No wallet. No charge cards. No drivers license. No voters registration. No identification at all except for her name typed in on a video store rental card. Little evidence that she was a citizen of this earth, much less a neighborhood on the West Side of Chicago. No proof that she belonged anywhere.

Monissa, the owner of the purse, was in the back seat of Cronin's unmarked squad car, weeping into her small hands. She didn't cry when Cronin led her by the elbow off a porch after he saw her drop some tin foiled packets as he drove by slow looking squarely at her. She didn't cry when he put her in the back seat of his car and found, at the bottom of her purse, more tin foil in neat one and a half inch squares, ready to wrap the dope in.

"I don't know why I have these," she said. "I just have it."

She didn't cry when she told her age--18--and that she had two babies already and one died, her second, a baby girl "born just this past March 22nd. She passed," she said real soft, "at two weeks old. They didn't tell me at the hospital that she was sick so I took

59

her home. She kept spitting up and then we took her back to the hospital and they said she had a hole in her heart. Then she just passed from me."

She didn't cry when she talked about dropping out of 11th grade after the second baby died…"I just didn't go back to school. I just didn't want to go no more." Or how she quit her job at Wendy's to take a GED course for a high school diploma and then when she got there, she was told the program was full, so she hasn't worked since.

She didn't cry when she talked about her someday dream to be a secretary and how she'd been practicing on her sister's typewriter but then the ink ribbon ran dry.

She didn't even cry when she told Cronin that her father left her when she was a little girl and "I ain't talked to him much since cause his phone is out." Or when she told him there was no water in the apartment that she and her boy friend and their first baby lived in down the street and that's why she and he were at this dope spot on Homan and Lexington when Cronin pulled up.

See, it was so her boy friend could wash up and put on a new Italian silk shirt he bought off the street and look fine on a Friday night that they were even in that place--an abandoned apartment on the first floor. She'd ironed a pair of pants for him and brought them over to him while he was washing up. She was just waiting for him on the front steps when Cronin came by.

"I don't know nothing about the dope business," she said. "I never been arrested before."

Monissa did not cry until Cronin left the car and came back with a 19 year old bare chested youth and sat him down hard in the back seat next to her. He had a silk shirt clutched in one hand.

"Is this your boy friend?" Cronin asked. Monissa looked up and it was then she started to cry.

"Is he …is he going to jail?"

"I asked you a question. Is this your boy friend?"

"Yes sir," she said collapsing against the young man's shoulder. She cried silently except for a few escaping sobs. The young man looked down at her huddled next to him but did not put his arm around her.

"Well, this asshole was trying to jump out of the window. What's he jumping out of the window for?"

"I don't know, sir," said Monissa. "He just there. Like me."

"I swear on my mama's grave....and my mama has passed...I was just washing up and I got scared when you drove up," said the boy friend. "I was washing up, you can smell me."

"I don't want to smell you and you're lying," said Cronin. "You were working this spot and you're lying."

"He don't work that spot, sir, and me neither," said Monissa.

"Then what's this?" asked Cronin, unwrapping the worn and folded up piece of paper that had been in her purse. "Duck...$5. Joanne...$10. Tony...$35. Netta...$10. What's this a list for? The Fuller brush man?"

"That's a list of somebody owe money," the boy friend said.

"Owe money for what?" asked Cronin.

The question was greeted by silence from the boy friend. Monissa looked up at him, stopped her crying and said nothing either.

"I'm taking her in. I'm charging her. She'll be out on an I-bond in the morning," said Cronin, starting the squad car.

"I just had three bags, that's all, sir," Monissa said quietly from the back seat. "I just had come out of the building. I don't sell no drugs, sir. A boy told me to hold it when he seen you coming. He gave it to me. That boy named May."

"You going to take me in too?" asked the boy friend.

"I'm going to take you in and name check you. Then if you are clear I'm going to let you go. But you know a lot of shit. If you are fair with me, I'll try to make it easier for her in court. I've got to charge her. I saw her drop it."

"I swear on my mama's grave I don't sell no drugs," said the boy friend. "I'll tell you where there are guns over on St. Louis. I'll tell you where they hide the dope over at the gas station on Homan. But on my mama...and my mama passed away in October...I don't sell from no spots. I was just washing up. Here, smell me, on my mama's grave."

"Oh, shut up," said Cronin, pulling his car into the alley behind the police station.

The boy friend's name check came back clear and he could go. So he suddenly had little to say about the guns on St. Louis or the drugs on Homan Avenue once it was clear there were no warrants out for him. He left the station in a hurry and did not look back at Monissa when he walked out. She was charged with possession of a controlled substance. She did not cry again until he left her alone in a grim-green interrogation room in the back of the noisy station. A few deep mournful cries escaped her mouth as she sat, her head bent down over her knees. Then she stopped and looked up, blinked the water out of her eyes and walked away toward the lock up, handcuffed and led by a female custodian.

The police laboratory came back several weeks later with a report that the bags Monissa had dropped from the porch were filled with dummy dope. They'd been selling $10 bags of fake heroin that night, a scam that can get you killed on the West Side. But scam or no scam, the charges against Monissa were dropped in court. Cronin never saw her on the street again.

A year later Cronin bumped into the boy friend in narcotics court. He was out on bond on a drug charge and hoping to beat it, he said. And the girl he was with that night at Homan and Lexington, Cronin asked. Oh, he didn't know much except that the girl was dead. He wasn't living with her anymore when her apartment caught on fire and she got trapped inside. He said he didn't know the details.

Monissa was 19 when she died. It is not known if she was buried next to her second born baby – the little one, who like her young mother, was born with a hole in her heart.

38 NEVER WENT FISHING

"If they ever kill me," he said one night toward the end of his life, "do you know what I want you to do, Cronin? I want you to say to all the gangbangers, 'You all know what? 38 told me everything you jerks.' That's what I want you to say, Cronie. "Let them know I was talking on them the whole time to you."

And Cronin said back, without looking at him because he was driving, "Okay, but you ain't dead yet. I've never seen you so nervous. You must be getting scared."

"Not scared, Cronin, smart. I'm getting old for what I'm doing. I'm 21. When I get shot up you ain't going to come over and stand in front of the hospital bed and say, 'I'm going to miss you'."

"No, I'm going to stand in front of the bed and say 'I told you so.'"

It was the last time Cronin and 38 would ever talk. The end was near although neither of them knew it that chill night, with the moon a cold sliver climbing up over the city--up early too, for hardly a star was out yet.

38 had beeped Cronin earlier that night and left his signature – 007 – which indicated the romantic way he saw his relationship with Cronin, that of a secret agent, which in many ways he was. Better think of one's self as secret agent than 'informant' or 'snitch'. On the streets, that was lower than a whore, worse than a dude who beat a woman, less honorable than wounding a baby during a drive-by shooting.

But he was an erratic secret agent. There were times he'd beep Cronin twice a night, three nights in a row. And then Cronin would call him back and they would agree to meet somewhere dark to talk and 38 would materialize out of the nowhere, slip into the back seat and after driving a few blocks Cronin would say:

"Okay 38. What do you know? And I mean what do you know that I don't know?"

And then there were many times after he beeped he didn't show up at all.

This night 38 showed up at the agreed place, in the alley behind his father's house, which he had been kicked out of. The squad car's lights were off and when it seemed all clear, 38 bounded over a six foot fence and slid into Cronin's car as quiet as a shadow.

"I come to give you your jacket back, man," said 38, handing over a beat up old grey parka.

"Hell, I thought I'd never see it again," said Cronin. "Just when I'm about to give up on ya 38, you surprise me."

"I'm full of surprises Cronie. I surprise myself. But nothing like the night I met ya Cronin. You surprised me. I owe you one....you could have shot me that night."

That night was five years before. 38 was just 17 and had a new job which he handled with the swagger of a kid in a new suit that fit just right. It was working security for one of Bo Diddley's dope spots on West Ohio Street – an apartment on the second floor – and 38 was to let no one through the door that shouldn't get through the door. They'd warned him when he began that night to look out for a certain cop who was popping up when you least expect him. He was a short white guy with brown hair, who yelled a lot and "didn't take no shit." They said his name was Cronie.

The night wasn't half over when there was a knocking on the door at the bottom of the stairs and 38, with gunslinger bravado, yelled out, "Who the fuck is it?" from the top of the stairs. He got only a mumbled answer back. The knock came again and 38 yelled a little louder. Still a mumble...

"What the...?"

38 went down the stairs and swung the door open wide, a loaded pistol in his hand pointed straight at the man standing there knocking. He was short and white and had brown hair. He also had a gun on his hip, handcuffs on his belt, a radio on his side, a flash light in his hand

and ....it wasn't the big bad wolf. It was worse. The guy was yelling big time and the words were, "PO-LICE!" 38 turned and ran back up the stairs. He'd just met Cronin.

"You could have shot me right there, Cronin," 38 remembered later. "I knew right then who you was 'cause they'd just been saying some scary shit about you. Bo Diddley and the older guys. "You could have shot me right through my head cause I had that gun pointed at you. But you didn't. You didn't even draw your gun."

"That's because you did the right thing," Cronin said. "You, the big fucking gang banger answered the door and your eyes got as big as two silver dollars and you ran up the stairs and dropped the gun."

"I like you for that, Cronin," 38 said."Cause I got so scared when I opened the door and there you was, looking so rough, like you was the po-lice..."

"I am the po-lice," Cronin said

"I know, but there were so many things I saw in you. I dropped that gun and ran. You looked like everything they was talking about, like a man who could do something to you if you didn't listen."

"Well, you listened back then and you didn't get goofy on me, did you? You didn't get shot, you got arrested."

"But I was young then Cronin and I got scared. Now you'd never get me dirty with a gun now. I'd run on you."

"You can run on me 38 but you can't run all your life. Eventually you are going to get tired like everyone does on the streets. I don't know what will ache first, your heart or your feet."

38 had the soft face of a boy child, a lean body and a languorous almost sotto voice that belied the stockade of fireworks exploding in his soul. He wore his hair in oiled curls, Chuck Berry style, and depending on the evening's agenda, he'd sometimes sport a jeweled stud in his nose. In the summer, he often wore his pants unbuttoned at the top so that they hung precariously off his slim hip bones, promising any second to fall to the ground.

"Out here, girls like this kind of thing," he would say with a grin.

38 had the stuff the West Side gangsters looked for in young boys like him. On the street they call it 'heart'--a recklessness toward life

and death that in the beginning, anyway, and for a few years, made 38 one of the more daring players.

He started off as a good soldier who would do what they wanted done but would not do themselves because it was too dangerous, too implicating and they could get their fingerprints dirty--like shooting up a car wash of an opposition drug dealer, breaking the arms of a fellow gang member who ran off with a couple of grams of the bosses' dope, or simply shooting a worker at some dope spot because his boss was stepping onto another's guy's turf and not paying off for the privilege.

In the beginning, 38 would go on these missions with a glee shivering inside him, a thrill running down his spine and not a moment's hesitation. He ripped and roared through the streets, his whole being rushed with the excitement of ambush, of carrying a hidden gun like the gunslingers on TV, going on secret missions like the 007 he saw himself to be. In the beginning, he was afraid of nothing. Not pain. Not death. Once he spat a bullet out of his mouth in a public washroom an hour after being shot in the head. He robbed the very Nigerian drug dealers he was working for. He smuggled drugs into the airport and into Cook County Jail. But toward the end, and he seemed to know he was nearing it, he developed one true phobia--a fear he openly admitted to Cronin.

"I do some weird things Cronin, and I ain't afraid of getting shot. But I can't handle jail for a damn."

"Then you better quit this Wild West shit," Cronin said, "'cause that's where you are going. You're a player in a dangerous game. There's no winners. I ain't seen one yet. You're going to jail, or you're going to die young, 38."

"I'll take dying young Cronin. I just can't stand being locked up."

38 already had been shot four times--twice in the head and twice in the knees. But he wore his scars like a sailor does tattoos -- to show he's been around. And he wore them without complaint. After that first encounter on Ohio Street, Cronin and 38 must have met a hundred times. It was a relationship based on a clear understanding of who the other was. Cronin was the cop who sat in the front seat. 38 was the gangbanger who sat in the back. They both knew the same people. They were both out on the street at night and both wanted to

know what the other was up to. 38 only told Cronin what he chose to tell him. Cronin listened and believed what he chose to believe.

"Sometimes I beep ya just to talk to ya Cronin," 38 said once. "Like the time I beeped you on Christmas, remember?"

"I remember," said Cronin. "But you beeped me to see what the fuck I was up to. You didn't beep me to say hello and how are you. Let's face it 38, you beep when you need something."

Looking back, Cronin remembers what 38 chose to tell him was always on the money.

"The ones I talk on are the ones I try to get out of my way, so I can get one step ahead of them," 38 told him. "See, you'll get them off the street so they can't ride up on me."

"I hear you," Cronin said.

"You want guns or dope?" 38 would say.

"Whatever will put the bad guys in jail," Cronin would answer.

"Okay, listen, you know that spot on Homan, the red house, I was just in there and they got..." and 38 would lean forward and start talking.

Never did 38 have any delusions that Cronin wouldn't arrest him if he was caught dirty. Talking in the back seat didn't give him a free pass. And never did Cronin think 38 wouldn't run on him if he was dirty. If they did collide in some alley or on a corner, which they often did, and 38 didn't split because he wasn't carrying something hot, which was seldom, 38 was sultry and Cronin was rough during their encounter. There was never a hint by either one --not even a meeting of the eyes-- that they'd talked many hours under dark shadows in a squad car. And his buddies never guessed that when they saw him sidle off sometimes and slip a quarter into a pay phone, it wasn't 38 beeping a fellow brother of the street. It was 007 calling Cronin.

After a while, Cronin could see a change in 38. He was just as wild, in fact wilder, thrashing around wild, but no longer so loyal and willing to follow orders when the gang chiefs ordered him around. He was getting in trouble with the very chiefs he was working for. The ones who picked him as one of their gunmen because he had 'heart.' Cronin found him up one night walking the street after he'd been badly beaten.

"What happened, you get in a fight? You look like a raccoon your eyes are so black and blue," said Cronin.

"I wasn't listening," said 38, his eyelids pouched and swollen and his head laid back on the seat of the car. "I'm not listening no more and I'm not going to listen," said 38.

"What does that mean?" asked Cronin.

'It mean if they tell me to go do something and I don't want to do it, I won't do it. I'll say yes, but if I see an 'out' door and soon as I see it, I'm going to run and you won't see me again. I can hide. I'm good at hiding."

"Not good enough," said Cronin. "You got a beating. What did you do to get this?"

"I was told to do something that..."

"Told to do what?" asked Cronin."

"Told to go shoot up and I didn't want to do it. We always asked to do things we don't want to do."

"Was it Willie? Did he tell you to do it?" asked Cronin."

"Yeah, and I said yeah I would do it. If I said no right there, you probably wouldn't see me today. If you did, I would be in the hospital..."

"Like your friend, Larry," said Cronin. "He wouldn't talk. I visited him in the hospital. He was messed up pretty bad. They broke both his legs, each one in three places. He wouldn't tell me who did it."

"They beat him with a tire iron cause he messed up," said 38.

"What did they want you to shoot up?" asked Cronin again.

"A car wash on Chicago Avenue and Pulaski, the Black Souls run it. You know they broke a brother up--Little Sam-- last summer with a baseball bat. And now when they want someone broken up, Willie get on the phone and he being in jail, he don't say 'go break'em up, or shoot'em if you have to' on the jail phone cause he know the guards are listening. He tell us to go visit them like 'Larry or Little Sam' and then he'll say,'I have nothing else to say' and that means I'm supposed to go and do what they did to Larry and Little Sam and..."

"Did PooPoo beat you up?" asked Cronin.

"No, he enforced it. He made sure it was done," said 38

"And you got beat because you didn't mess someone up?" asked Cronin.

"No, Cronin. Because I'm not listening, that's all. I'm not listening."

No doubt, 38 was getting disillusioned with the danger game. Sure he liked the ducking and dodging action, the titillation of the street at night, the cold heavy weight of a loaded gun tucked inside his pants and the flush of power that went with it. But the danger game went both ways. One night he would be the big game hunter he saw himself to be, prowling the streets, following the scent, riding high with his buddies in a fast car down Washington Boulevard, his finger on the trigger. But the next night, he would be the prey, laying low, covering his tracks and running for dear life on foot because whoever he was stalking yesterday played the same game.

One early evening, when Cronin spotted him walking alone, his stone washed jeans and jacket looking like they'd been on him for two days, 38 climbed in the back of Cronin's squad after Cronin patted him down, and said, "Don't worry. I ain't going to run because I'm tired. I been on my feet and I'm tired. I been working hard. I been fighting all day."

"Hell, you guys don't fight. You shoot."

"I don't do that Cronin, you never seen me do that. I've shot at people but just to be playing."

"Do you consider shooting at people to be just playing?" Cronin said.

"No man, but that's how we played when we was young," 38 said.

"And you're not young now?" said Cronin.

"No, I'm an old player," said 38, "I get tired."

Slowly it was sinking in to 38 that as an enforcer on the street, as a hired gun for the gang chiefs, as a foot solider for the Vice Lord army, it was not getting him anywhere. He was no better off than the day he met Cronin at the bottom of the stairs on West Ohio Street when he was 17. He had no house, no apartment, no car, no credit card, no credit, no insurance, no bank account and no jewelry except the stud he wore in his nose. His toil went for the gang: "the mob" 38 called them. Yet the spoils, the thousands of dollars of dope money pouring in every day, money 38 often helped collect, went to a few who bought themselves floor length mink coats and strutted around late night lounges letting the furry hems skim the booze-soaked cigarette butts on the floor tiles while they shot pool and their entourage of cars sat double parked outside on Madison Street, their 17 year old drivers waiting faithfully behind the wheel.

They were sacrificing kids like him. He knew it. He'd been seeing it. If you picked up a dope habit, they dropped you. If you got caught and went to jail, they wrote you off. If you got killed, they forgot your name. There were a hundred more 38's waiting as replacements in the wings. The gang chiefs merely waggled their finger and said,'Next'.

38 got more daring-- he delivered heroin and cocaine to his gang chief who was locked up in Cook County jail. He'd give it to a county jail guard who Willie, his chief, had paid off and from there Willie would distribute it as favors inside the jail, trying to elicit loyalty from the baby brothers who'd gotten caught. 38 would walk right into the criminal courts building with it on him.

He stole a drug dealer's car one night simply because he felt like it. When the car phone rang he answered it and it was the owner telling him to bring the damn car back or else. 38 ran the car into a curb, blew a tire and left it.

He started hanging around with Nigerians and doing his own thing. He became the conduit between the Nigerian white heroin suppliers on the north side and the drug dealers on the West Side. He'd get a percentage of the deal when it went down. And he spent it all and he couldn't even tell you on what. He also became their leg man. The Nigerians would give him a belt filled with heroin which he would strap around his waist under his shirt and a car would pick him up on a corner, drive him halfway to the south side, drop him off and he'd run through a gangway to another waiting car that would take him to Midway Airport. There he would go into the public washroom, meet another Nigerian who was waiting there and then transfer the belt. The Nigerian would then board the plane for LA with no fear of going through customs since it was a domestic flight.

The system worked well. But life on the streets was catching up on him. He was gasping for breath and feeling old.

"Let's go fishing, Cronie. Take me fishing," 38 said when he climbed into Cronin's squad car for their last long talk and he gave Cronin his grey parka back, a parka Cronin had loaned him when he got out of prison and it was cold outside and no one in his family or from his gang would give him something warm to wear.

But Cronin didn't want to talk about fishing. Cronin didn't fish anyway. The one time he went out on Lake Michigan to go salmon fishing his face turned as grey as the waves and he stayed closed to the gunnels, in case he needed to bend over the side. Cronin wanted to talk about the guns 38 said he knew about when he beeped him. The Cat lady's guns. The Cat lady with the rifles stored up and under her couch--"rifles that shoot long bullets," 38 had told him.

"How many times you seen these guns?" Cronin asked.

"Once last night. She is storing them for two guys.

"How many guns are up there?" asked Cronin.

"'bout six or seven," said 38.

"If I went there tonight, do you think they would be there?" asked Cronin.

"Only if I be there first and make sure they are there. I can get in there anytime I want...."

"Now, I don't want to front you off. Can you get in there, check the guns, get out and let me know so we can go in but not look like you had anything to do with it?"

"Sure Cronin. If I said I can do it I can do it for you. I'm not a coward."

"I know that 38, I'm not saying you are. I'm saying let's do it right."

"Okay. Let's go get'em. But I'd rather go fishing, Cronin. Let's go to the lakefront. I'd like to go fishing with you."

"Tell me about the god damn guns. I got to know they are there," said Cronin.

"If I said they are there, they are there," said 38. "We'll go fishing all right," said Cronin. "If those guns ain't there, I'll use you as bait."

38 laughed. He liked talk like that.

"If you won't take me fishing, get me a job Cronin, you got clout," said 38. "Let's rent a boat and go out on the lake. I gotta get out 'a here."

"What have you done? You gone goofy again? You like ripping and running too much. You're a wild boy, 38. If the police don't catch up with you, the streets will, or maybe they already have."

"I need a job, Cronin. I need to go fishing. There's going to be a war out here this summer. I want to be off the streets during this time."

"You couldn't hold down a job, 38. Not for 8 hours," said Cronin.

"Maybe that way I could find a different crowd to hang with so's I won't be here when...."

"When what, 38?" said Cronin. "I been telling you 38 for how long now? What have I been telling you, ya goof? There's no winners in your game."

"A lot of people be on dope now, the young ones. They going straight onto white heroin. And a lot of people sticking up for dope money and certain gang members are coming out of the penitentiary and they are bringing the gang laws from the joint out to the street and there's going to be a blood bath. I don't want to be here Cronin, let's go fishing. Let's go way out on the lake so far out we can't see the city."

"No," said Cronin. "Let's do the guns. You go check them out and then beep me. We'll talk about fishing later."

38 got out of the car, acting skittish.

"Don't look up at the moon, it might make you goofy," said Cronin.

"I never look up," said 38, "I just watch my back."

Then he disappeared like a gazelle down the street. Cronin waited for hours but he never got beeped. The cat lady got to keep her guns and 38 never went fishing.

POST SCRIPT: It wasn't long afterwards that 38 smashed out the windows in his father's house and there was a warrant for his arrest and then Cronin heard that 38 had left town. An ATF agent in Milwaukee, Wisconsin rang Cronin up during the summer of 1992. He'd been talking to a kid named "38" who said he knew Mike Cronin from Gang Crimes in Chicago and he was just checking to see if it was true.

"Yeah I know him," said Cronin "Does he want to talk to me?"

"No," said the agent. "He says he is scared of you."

He'll be back, thought Cronin. If he doesn't catch a case and get locked up, he'll be back on the West Side. Up to the same old shit. Playing the danger game. The only game 38 knows.

One summer night Cronin would catch a wink of his shadow running from him down the street. Or the goof would beep him cause he needed something and he'd put in the old 007 as a message. But 38 never did. Before summer could lean down close and breath her warm wet breath through the streets, 38 had fled the city. He told Keith, his half brother, to take an insurance policy out on his life. He wasn't going to live the year out, he said. His brother never did, even though he knew there were people on the street looking for 38 to kill him. All sorts of people. 38 missed the bloodbath of the summer of '92 in Chicago. It was the second deadliest year for homicides in the city's history and the West Side, the place he called home, was right at the top with death statistics. In the autumn, he called his father's house long distance and, in 38's fashion, didn't say much except to tell them that he'd met a girl in Milwaukee, she'd just inherited some property down south, that he had come down to Mississippi with her and they were going to get married.

"It seemed like he thought he was going to begin his life over again," said his brother. "He didn't invite us down for it or nothing. I don't even remember where in Mississippi he was. But he said he was getting married and we couldn't believe it. And I was wondering, what was he doing to that town? He was always a time bomb about to go off. You ever met someone you felt you never knew? That was my brother. You could be talking to him, turn your head for a second, look back and he'd be gone--like he was never there and when he was, you never knew who he was."

The end came not when 38 was dodging down an alley, leaping bullets. Not scaling a ten foot fence which he did better than anybody else around St. Louis and Lake Street. Not jumping garage roofs and winning the foot race against the police or hitting the gas pedal in some hot car. The end of the game did not come on the West Side or on any big city streets. It came on November 6, 1992 in a small town in Mississippi during the morning quiet, while he was still in bed, asleep, his guard down. At 8:15 a.m. 38 was shot five times while his eyes were still closed. It was his wedding day, less than two hours before he was to be married.

His bride was charged with his murder because he had beaten her up the night before. But the rumor on the street was that it was probably the girl's brother or her old man who killed him, not liking his city slick ways and his wildness and the meanness he brought down from the north. Whatever, 38 died the year he knew he would, under strange circumstances, with mystery clouding the truth. Cronin was not surprised. And probably, 007 would have liked it that way.

I'M A NUT BUT I'M ME TONIGHT

Drozd was on the front sidewalk looking up and Cronin had gone 'round the alley and he was in the back yard looking up, waiting for his eyes to adjust to the dark. They were both looking up to a second floor apartment over an empty, dusty-windowed H and R Block office, closed now that tax time had passed. A light was on upstairs, one unadorned bulb glowing solidly from the ceiling.

This was a smoke house, one of hundreds in their purview, and they'd hit it just last week without glorious results. Before they and their fellow officers could gallop up the stairs to the second floor, both back and front stairs simultaneously, and get through the doors, anyone and everyone with any dope on them had ducked quickly out the second floor window and disappeared across the roof tops like urban mountain goats.

Here at LeClair and Chicago Avenue, the buildings were shoulder to shoulder and made for escape. Though it was still cold out, a window in the apartment always sat lifted. It didn't need a sign marked EXIT.

Cronin went quietly up the steps of the back porch, careful not to trip over the extension cord that snaked from an adjacent building basement, curled up the steps and squeezed through the second floor back door he wanted to enter. Pirated electricity. But that was not uncommon nor his concern. He tried hard not to make the porch planks creak under his weight. He got to the second floor without the stairs giving him away. Then he banged on the door. Drozd heard it from where he stood and headed up the steep and narrow front stairway that led to the second floor. No answer. Cronin kept banging and shouted, "Po-lice." Suddenly, with no sound of quick shuffling or re-arranging inside, the door opened slightly and Anthony, the caretaker, peered out at him with his one good eye.

"This time, there ain't nobody here but me," he said, grinning.

"Yeah, right. Are you going to open the door?" said Cronin.

"Of course," said Anthony. "Come on in. You're Cronie. You were here last week."

"And I'm back again," he said. "Now open the front door. I got a friend who wants to get in."

Anthony clumped over to the front door, let Drozd in, and then collapsed resigned into a cheap metal kitchen chair, rolling his one good eye. Cronin and Drozd roved through the place, which was a topsy-turvy collection of four rooms with overturned chairs, some stained couches with old shoes sticking out from the cushions and piles of clothes, thrown into corners as casually as garbage in an alley.

In the kitchen, the stove had all its burners on but there was nothing cooking. Spill had hardened down the edges of the stove and turned into rivulets of dark rock, as if once, in another millennium, there's been an eruption from some boiling pot that had never been wiped up. Anthony was unconcerned, leaning back in his chair against what appeared to be a pantry door.

"What's in there?" asked Cronin.

"You don't want me to open it," said Anthony, nodding his head knowingly.

"Why not?" said Cronin, reaching over Anthony's head and rattling the door handle which wouldn't open.

The sound of savage growling erupted, followed by mournful yelps and painful howls. Animal nails scratched at the wood. The door thumped with the weight of large animal bodies hungry for an attack.

"Don't worry. They locked in," said Anthony, with a smile." I only open the door to feed them."

"What have you got in there, wolves?" asked Cronin.

"No," said Anthony, unmoved by the frenetic barking at his back, "just two Dobermans. I keep them instead of a gun."

Drozd was in what would have been a bedroom, had there been a bed, a chest, a mirror on the wall, an alarm clock and some pictures at the bedside, even a pillow and sheet. But there was nothing but years of litter scattered about and a cheap wall to wall carpet that was soggy. In the closet, hidden under a pile of filthy worn-once clothes, he found a brand new safe, riveted solidly to the floor.

"What's in this fucking safe?" shouted Drozd, from the closet.

"Don't know nothing about it," said Anthony.

"The hell you don't," said Cronin. "What's this then?" and he pointed to two busted up tables sitting in what was meant to be the living room. They were a clutter with razors, broken mirrors, bottles of alcohol and glass smoking pipes. Cronin smashed the pipes with his flash light as he spoke. Anthony winced.

"This is a smoke house officer, I provide a service, you know that," said Anthony. "Just nobody here right now."

"If I find any dope here asshole, you are going to jail."

"You won't," said Anthony, relaxing back into his kitchen chair. "It's an off-night and I got no dope. I'm clean tonight. They bring it and smoke it here. Just no business tonight."

But other nights, he went on to say proudly, other nights he did good business. This was a week night. They are slow sometimes. But on a Friday night, he could get 8 to 10 people who would pay $10 a person just to come in off the street and, in privacy, get a room to turn their powder cocaine into rock and then smoke it. One hundred dollars a Friday night just for them to sit there. That paid the bills. The rent, which was $300 a month, he paid with his disability check.

"I get disability because I am a nut," said Anthony, as the two policemen continued to rummage through the clutter. "I been in and out of nut houses for the last 12 years."

"How do you know you are a nut?" said Drozd, as he walked into the kitchen holding a paper bag he was going to look through and then deposit in a corner where all the other trash had been thrown.

"Because I have split personalities," said Anthony, with some pride and aiming the glance of his good eye at Drozd who was no longer looking at him or listening to him. "I am two people. I have another ego. His name Quincy and he don't smoke 'caine. He live on the South side."

"So who are you now?" asked Cronin.

"I'm me."

"Which me?"

"I'm Anthony from the West Side who run a smoke house."

"Well," said Drozd, "when are you not you?"

"Well, when I'm the other guy," said Anthony. "I leave the West Side and go south and when I cross 85th Street, I become Quincy and he don't run a smoke house and he don't use no 'caine."

"Yeah, but how do we know you are really you tonight and not him?" asked Cronin.

"Well look at my face," said Anthony. "It's me."

Cronin and Drozd groaned and headed for the front door. The squad car was down in front.

"But if you met 'me' on the south side," he was saying as they were leaving, "I wouldn't be me. I'd be him --Quincy-- and you wouldn't be knocking on my door then...cause Quincy don't run no smoke house and Quincy don't do no 'caine and..."

They lost the rest of what he was mumbling when they pulled away. Two weeks later, Anthony staggered into the emergency room of Loretto Hospital, just blocks down from his smoke house. He'd been hit over the head with a bottle and his skull was cracked open. He was bleeding heavily and the blood rolled down over the closed eye lid of his bad eye and pooled in its recesses and congealed on the lashes. Before they took him in to get stitched up, a nurse bent down and asked him some questions. He didn't tell her he was a nut. He just handed her his Medicare card. And when she asked his name he didn't say, "It's me." He said, "My name Quincy." But he wasn't on the South side and he was very far away from 85th Street.

A BLOW AND A SLICE

"It's the pizza man. Son of a bitch, the mobile pizza man. And look where he's set up shop!"

Cronin and Drozd pulled up at the corner of Cicero and Congress, where a crowd had congregated. It was Friday. Pay day. Everyone was in a spending mood, ready to buy a blow of heroin. And one of their first stops was this corner, where they sell dope on the street. Walk up, drive up, limp up, stagger up curb service. Just say the right word, slip a ten into the hand of some sixteen year old runner and the night, or at least the next few hours is lost in a carefree snort of forgetfulness or bliss or rage--whatever mood your heroin high happens to pursue. No overhead for this business operation. No sales taxes. No light bills. No insurance. No social security for the employees. No rent. No advertising. No equal opportunity. No money back guarantee. Just pure cash. No notes. No checks. No credit. And no questions.

Behind the rear wheel of the abandoned school bus that sat there sinking into an empty lot is where they were stashing the bags of heroin this night. Or maybe they were handing it out the broken basement window of that greystone two flat, or perhaps it was in a paper bag stuffed into that old metal barrel near the curb that always had a fire burning in it during winter. Or perhaps, some kid was carrying it in the crotch of his pants out there in the alley. It always changed to confuse the police and avert a stick-up by some neighborhood addict who wanted the dope and didn't have the money or wanted the money so he could buy some dope.

The circle is round and small on the West Side. When Cronin and Drozd rolled up, stopped the squad in the middle of the street and got out, the congenial jabber of everybody sharing a public secret quieted. Nobody was suddenly doing anything. There were blank looks on fifty faces. Like people claiming they were waiting to buy a ticket to the movies but there was no ticket window and no movie.

It was pretend. It was a game of who's fooling who. The answer was nobody. And everybody knew it.

A postal employee, still in uniform, meandered away from the curb over to the pizza truck. The teen age boy he was talking to started walking nonchalantly down the alley, afraid to look back. The sea of people parted as the two policemen walked through the crowd. A CTA bus driver, also in uniform, stayed in one spot and did not move, flirting intensely with a girl on the curb but his eyes were not on her. They followed, instead, the movement of the two plain clothed cops, which was not easy, since they split and went two different ways.

"So we don't have just one entrepreneur here on this corner, that fucking High Nif who's selling this dope, now we got two...the pizza man" said Cronin.

The pizza man heard him mutter and looked up with a dizzy smile. He was Puerto Rican and he understood everything except the word 'entrepreneur'. His truck said "Luigi's Pizza" on the side and he was doing one whale of a business, selling one-slice- at-a-time, eat-as-you-walk-outta-here-with-a-dime-bag pizza.

"That's how busy this drug corner is," said Cronin." The pizza man has opened up shop. While they are buying dope, he is selling pizza to them. They say there is no economy on the West Side. Shit there's an economy out here. It's based on drugs. The clothes, the rent, the cars, the food money – all dependent on drugs – like our pizza man here."

He turned toward the back of the truck, where the pizza man had the side up and steaming pizza sat sliced and waiting.

"How long you been coming here?" he asked the pizza man.

"I been coming every night for almost a week now. Big crowd. But I get outta here when it get dark. It no safe here at night."

"No kidding." said Cronin. "How long you going to keep coming?"

"All summer if the people still here. You think they will be?"

"Not if I can help it." said Cronin.

"Then I find another corner out here," said the pizza man, still smiling.

"I'm sure you will."

Cronin shook his head in disgust at Drozd and turned around. "That's good," he said. "Come here for a blow and a slice. That's good."

"You want one, a slice?" said the pizza man, detecting the policeman's anger and venturing a few feet away from his truck to offer Cronin a piece of pizza he held on a sheet of waxed paper in his right hand. "You the police. For you it is free."

"No thanks," said Cronin.

"Then come back, maybe another time," said the pizza man.

"I'll be back," said Cronin. "But it's not because I like pizza."

THEY DIDN'T TELL ME WHO I KILLED.

Cronin knew the spot but he didn't know the kid. The spot he'd been in before. It was on the first floor, apartment on the right, and had a handwritten sign posted next to the door that said: "No begging. No sweating. Pipes $5." It was a smoke house where people paid to get in and smoke cocaine. The kid was outside near the gangway leading to the front steps, hanging with a group of three or four others, probably lookouts, who started to cower when Cronin and his partner, Drozd, drove up. But this one particular kid didn't move. He looked dumbly at them driving up and getting out of the car.

"What's up, my man?" The kid was huge. He easily outweighed the two of them together and he naively kept his hands in the pockets of his sweat pants.

"Take your hands out of your pocket," said Cronin, who then patted him down. Drozd was patting down the others. They were clean, of course, being lookouts. But the two policemen couldn't figure out this kid. He didn't have an attitude. He just stood there, like a tree.

"What's your name, homie?" asked Cronin.

"B-B-B-B-B-Brian," the big kid answered.

"What's your street name?"

"B-B-B-B-B-Brian." The kid stuttered.

"What are you doing here?" asked Cronin.

"St-st-st-anding here. I j-j-just got out," said the kid.

"When?" said Cronin.

"Two days ago," said the kid.

"Let's name check you. Get in the car," said Cronin.

The kid gave no resistance and ducked his hulk into the back seat and sat, rubbing the top of his thighs slowly and looking around at the squad car he was sitting in.

"What were you in for, my man?" asked Cronin.

"Cr-cr-criminal sexual assault and manslaughter," said the kid.

"Who'd you kill?" asked Cronin, turning around to look more closely at this giant in his back seat.

"They didn't t-t-t-t-ell me who I killed. It was a g-g-g-girl but I didn't know her name. They didn't t-t-tell me."

"Shit," muttered Cronin, calling in the kid's name to radio dispatch to see if he was wanted on a warrant.

"How tall are you?" asked Cronin.

"Uhhhhh, maybe f-f-f-five ten," said the kid, not knowing.

"Shit, you are taller than that. You got to be over six feet. How much do you weigh?"

"D-d-d-don't know," said the kid.

"Well, you got the look, the build from the joint. How long you been lifting weights?"

"Th-th-the whole time I was in prison. Since I was seventeen. That's all I done. Didn't get in no trouble. Just lifted weights."

"How much can you bench press?" said Cronin, looking at the kid's biceps which were as wide as a thigh.

"Four hundred and eighty five pounds," the kid answered, without a stutter.

"Man," said Cronin, slapping his palm against his forehead.

Just then the radio came back to Cronin. The kid was clear of warrants. He was clean. Cronin could let him go.

The kid sat there, not impatient to leave. He was looking out the window at the spot where he'd been standing. None of his buddies were there waiting for him. The place had emptied out.

"Where are you staying?," asked Cronin.

"I be-be-be laying my head with my grandmother, if I find where she live," said the kid. "My ma-ma-mama be dead. She died of an overdose while I was doing my time and my grandmother moved since she wrote to me in prison."

"Well, you can go. But don't be hanging here. You're on parole. And this is a dope spot so I don't want to catch you here again," said Cronin.

"I-I-I-I don't want no trouble," said the kid. "I just got out."

"I know," said Cronin. "Just stay off this fucking corner. Go home. Straight home."

The kid got out of the car and started to walk. The squad pulled slowly off, cruising toward the other spots in the same block. Cronin didn't look back. But if he had, he would have seen the big kid stop at the corner, step off the curb, step back again, shuffle his feet and look around-- searching in the dark for a direction. Then he just stood there like a tree. He really didn't have a home to go to.

WAITING TO GET LET IN

At first, they didn't see anything but the dark of the gangway. Then, as their eyes adjusted, they discerned a dark form on the pavement outside the basement door. Like a dog. A very large dog. But it wasn't barking. And it wasn't moving. And then Grapes tripped on it.

"Holy shit, it's not a dog. It's a man. He's dead."

"He ain't dead. That's my brother-in-law," said Skipper.

Skipper was being led by the policemen back to a side door into the basement where he lived. "We don't let him inside, he's a junkie and he steal from everybody in the house. So he sleep out here."

Skipper stepped over his brother-in-law's body and opened the door. The policemen -- Cronin, Grapes and Baby Face-- looked down on the cold cement and saw a man whose face was barely visible, rolled up, over and over, like a Cuban cigar, in an old rug. He was sleeping. They'd stopped Skipper a block from the house as he was driving away and showed him a search warrant for his apartment. They'd gotten a tip that he was holding drugs and guns for a near-by drug spot.

Skipper was living with his girl friend, her three kids, and her brother who just got out of the Army. Skipper was only 19 but he was a drug dealer. He returned with them, reluctantly, and opened the metal side door. They all walked in and down the stairs into the basement. It was cold and smelled of mildew. The three kids who belonged to Skipper's girl friend were sitting on a saggy sofa shoved up against the wall. They had no shoes on and were skimpily dressed. They stayed sitting there and didn't move. The cops looked around.

87

There were holes in the walls the size of your fist, "rat sized," Cronin thought, that were stuffed with old rags. The holes were right next to the kids' mattress, which was on the floor. A few of the rags had been pushed out. This was not a basement family room. This is what old folks called the cellar--a place where you stored things, not people.

The girl friend's parents owned the house and lived upstairs, distancing themselves from the goings on below. The policemen searched the cushions of some old chairs, looked under the sofa, through boxes, piles of clothes on the floor, under a mattress, checked the ceiling, perused the top of the refrigerator and behind the stove, but all they found were piles of bullets and $500. No guns and no dope.

The informant was wrong, or lying or he'd been right and they were too late. Dope and guns are hot commodities in the drug trade and they move fast and elusively, from one hiding place to another.

The $500 was curious since Skipper had no job. He could not explain it other than to say, "That money is mine."

"So you can't tell us how you made this money?" said Cronin.

"Nope," said Skipper.

Confident now that the police had nothing on him, he wasn't talking.

"You live in a fucking basement, you got a woman here with three kids that need supporting and she doesn't have a job. Her brother just got out of the Army and he's got no job, and you've got no job but you got $500 and you ain't saying where it came from."

"Nope, it's mine, that's all," said Skipper.

"Since we know where it came from, whether we found the dope tonight or not, why don't we just take it and give it to your girlfriend and have her go buy some shoes for the kids and some clothes. And maybe pay somebody to plaster up those rat holes near the kid's bed and fix this place up . How does that sound? You like that idea?"

"No, I don't," said Skipper. "That's my money."

"I didn't think you would," said Cronin, giving him back the stack of bills.

Though the police left empty handed, Skipper was not. The five hundred was already tucked into his back pocket as they closed the basement door. They stepped over the brother-in-law in the gangway. He hadn't moved. For the three gang crimes cops, the night's adventure had nothing to do with what they got, it was what they saw. The dope they thought was there wasn't there that night. But the product of that dope was. It was right under their feet-- rolled up in a rug, waiting like a dog to be let in.

MR. PEABODY NEVER LEARNED
HOW TO WHISTLE

The kid said they were doing it over there in the old garage, across the alley with the hand painted sign, hanging crooked from a rusted nail, that announced in a child-like scrawl: C and S AUTO REPAIR.

"They selling in there," said the kid. "And it go all night."

"Then we'll have to pay them a visit," said Cronin.

It was late afternoon and the West Side was still bright with golden sunlight. No chance to watch the garage and not be spotted. Kids were underfoot everywhere, mamas had moved kitchen chairs out on the stoops, middle aged men filled the corners of empty lots, lounging on old car seats, drinking that odd mixture of Cool Aid and cheap wine they called Shake an' Bake and sharing a lot of laughs. Cronin would get his buddies from Gang Crimes, Baby Face and Grapes, to come back with him later that night and see just how much business this garage was doing. If it was going good, they'd hit it.

It was June 21st and it took a long time for the sun to go down. It left reluctantly, backing down over the horizon slowly, burning bright orange as it departed, trying for one last peek at all the action it would miss between dark and dawn. On cue, the lightening bugs came out to take its place, blinking their iridescent bellies merrily at the night as they danced over the chain link fences and played hide-and-seek down the gangways.

An uneasy quiet began to settle in over the neighborhood. Once it was dark there rose the steady hum of unseen movement. Faces in windows, figures in gangways, silhouettes in the empty lots. Even the shadows seemed to emit a sound.

Overheard a jet roared low toward O'Hare Airport, its portholes ablaze in the sky, the passengers just finishing up their Scotch, pushing their seats upright, oblivious in their comfort that they were flying over some of the most dangerous terrain in America.

The night had settled in. The three policemen, Cronin, Baby Face and Grapes, had parked a half block away and walked quickly, their flashlights off. They walked through the gangway of a two flat and stood in it's back yard, motionless, watching "C and S AUTO REPAIR" from across the alley. It was very dark. The street light in the alley had been shot out, to their advantage. They walked to the fence gate at the back of the yard and climbed over rather than open it for it was rusty and anxious to squeak.

Once in the alley, they crossed over it and came up behind the garage, which was wooden and old and had gaps between the planks. Through the gaps, they could see the shadow of a man sitting attentively before the muffled grey light of a black and white television set.

He was watching Nelson Mandela who was standing before the United Nations. Cronin went and knocked on the side door of the garage, adjacent to the alley. The man inside emitted a nondescript response, a half grunt, half growl, letting whoever was at the door know that there was somebody inside but he wasn't saying who. It was a warning as well as an answer, for it could be anybody knocking on that door...a stickup man. Or the police.

Baby Face watched the man through the cracks. He was looking at the door where Cronin was knocking from the other side but he was not answering. Cronin wasn't saying the right words. He was supposed to be putting in an order. So he didn't open the door.

Cronin came back behind the garage to whisper to Baby Face. As he did, a woman emerged from the shadows, coming quietly along the back walk from a house on West Polk Street. She came to the side door of the garage, knocked, whispered and the door opened wide. She walked in and didn't close the door behind her. Cronin bolted for the open door. His flash light hit the chain links on the fence and clanked. An outside dog next door began to bark.

Inside, they must not have heard him for the door didn't slam shut. Cronin walked in through it and said, "Well, well, what have we here?"

The grey haired man, who'd been manning the place, stood and put his hands in the air without being asked. The woman, in her twenties, shrieked in surprise and collapsed, like an actress on cue, down on her back upon a filthy mattress that lay on the oily garage floor. She began to pant, "Oh God," with both hands clutched over her left breast. Grapes and Baby Face came in behind Cronin. Ted Koppel was interviewing Mandela. They flicked the TV set off and started looking around, using their flashlights as guides.

"You got nothing on me," the woman said, recovering quickly. "I'm dead serious. Search me. We ain't doing nothing here but watching TV."

"Sit down," she was told.

"You ain't got nothing on me," she said, sitting up.

Just then there was a knock on the garage door. Three taps. The police hadn't been there thirty seconds.

"Who's there? What do ya want?" Baby Face said, leaning into the wood of the garage door.

"I want three boys," was the answer from outside.

"Who is it, man?" said Baby Face.

"It's Smitty," was the answer. Three ten dollar bills came through a slot in the door. Baby Face took the money, opened the door and stood there, six feet tall with a gun on his hip.

"C"mon in," he said.

"Oh...shit!" said the customer. He was a white kid, in a janitor's uniform. For a moment he was paralyzed.

"Take your money and get out of here," said Baby Face.

"I don't want my money..I don't want it," and he started to run.

Baby Face leaned out and threw the money on the ground.

"Pick up your money and don't come back," he said.

Inside the garage, everyone was laughing, including the old man. He was still chuckling when the policemen found brown heroin and several hundred dollars on the mattress. There were 10 bags.

"Is this all you got?" asked Cronin who looked next to the TV and spotted a bottle of 'Dorman.' "You mixing here too?"

The man didn't answer.

"What are you doing this for old man, you use heroin?"

"Yeah," said the man.

"When's the last time you had a job?"

"Oh," said the man, thinking. "It was 1980 something. Working for Brach's candy. I was throwing chocolate into a big ole vat."

There was another knock on the door. Baby Face took the order, but before the money could slide through the slot, he opened the door. The man at the door had a work shirt on that said, "University of Illinois." He stepped back two steps and looked as if he were about to faint.

"See how easy it is to lose your job?" he said. "Don't come back here no more."

"Thank you." The man gasped and turned to run.

"I just come from my grandma's house. I swear," said the woman. "I just came to borrow $10 from Mr. Peabody here."

No one was listening to her. Mr. Peabody was sitting on the mattress next to her, talking to himself and eyeing a half empty bottle of cheap wine that was within arm's reach.

"Mr. Cronie. Please, sir. Mr. Cronie. I'm only 25. I just got out April 25th for forgery, Mr. Cronie. Credit card forgery..."

Another knock on the door. Baby Face leaned into the door and told the man on the other side who was mumbling to say "the password."

"What is it?" said the customer, confused.

"It's Yabba-dabba-do," said Baby Face.

"Yabba-dabba-do?" said the man, incredulous.

"I'm serious. Say it straight, man," said Baby Face.

"Yabba-dabba-do," said the man and Baby Face opened the door. The man ran all the way down the alley and turned right without looking back.

"Listen, you are all going to jail," said Cronin once the door closed. "This is too active a spot."

The woman began to whine and cry. "Oh please, Mr. Cronie. I just got out.."

"Come here a minute," said Cronin, taking her outside.

"How much time did you do?" he asked.

"Two years and nine months."

"Well, you got the cutting agent here, you got the blenders, you got ten bags here so where is the rest stored?" asked Cronin.

"Well, I wouldn't know that, sir," she said.

"Don't bullshit me. You are on parole..."

"Mr. Peabody is broke. He's just getting back on his feet. He ain't selling very much, sir. A gram is only $375. It's brown heroin--tar dope--he don't keep but 20 bags and when he run out, he re-cop, he ain't making that much money."

"Where is the dope coming from, who brings it?" Cronin said, pressing her.

"I really can't say, sir."

"Wrong. You CAN say but you WON'T say," said Cronin, taking her back into the garage and closing the door.

Again, another knock.

"What's up?" said Baby Face.

"You got brown?" asked the customer from the outside.

"What's the password?" said Baby Face.

"They didn't have a password last time I come here."

"What's your name?"

"Bubba."

"The password is Yabba-dabba-do," said Baby Face.

"Okay, yabba-dabba-do," said the customer, playing the game.

"No, I don't like that password," said Baby Face, pausing. "Hey, the new pass word is Cronin."

"Cronin?" said the voice in disbelief.

"Yeah, how's that?"

"I don't like that at all."

"Why don't you like that?" said Baby Face opening the door.

"Cause I heard that name before," said the man who then banged through the fence gate, out into the alley and cut through a back yard. Baby Face closed the door again.

"This may sound stupid but what's the whistle for..." Cronin asked Peabody who'd just told him he'd been using heroin for 20 years since he got out of the penitentiary. "I mean this whistle is in your bag of goodies." He held up a cheap carry-on bag.

"Well, my nephew had left it and I just had it. No particular reason. But you know, they do a lot of whistling around here and I can't whistle."

"What do you need to whistle for?" asked Grapes.

"They whistles when the police is out and I'm 45 years old...too old to learn how to whistle," said Peabody.

"Yeah," said Cronin. "You are 45 going on 82."

"My grandmother is 70 and she look good," said the girl, who was back sitting on the mattress.

"Did she use dope?" asked Grapes.

"Nope."

"Then neither of you are going to look like your grandma," said Cronin. "Okay, we better go. Do you want a last drink before we go, Peabody?"

"Appreciate it," said Peabody, reaching for the half pint sitting on a tool table next to a book called Adventures In Reading.

"Who's learning how to read?" asked Baby Face.

"Me," said the girl.

"You know what, Mr. Cronie. Life out here in the ghetto is so boring and so depressing," said Peabody, taking a swig. "Can I finish the rest?" he said emptying the bottle down his throat, not waiting for an answer.

"Depressing? Of course it is depressing when you use dope," said Cronin.

"Why do you think I do it," said Peabody, wiping his mouth.

"Why did you do it 20 years ago?" asked Cronin.

"Well," said Peabody, wiping his hands on his pants and tossing the bottle into a corner. "It was just something I was going to experiment with."

"If you ain't got no fucking job and you ain't got no money, why the fuck do you use dope?" said Cronin.

"Cause life is so depressing, Mr. Cronie," said Peabody.

"How much you spend a day on dope?" asked Grapes.

"Well..I'd say $200 a day," said Peabody.

"How can you say you are poor and depressed and spend $200 a day on dope?" said Cronin. "Peabody, if you had all the money you spent every day for the last 20 years, you could have built a big fucking house in the suburbs...."

The three policemen stood there, ready to go to the station.

"Oh, please don't send me back to prison. I only come here to borrow $10," said the girl, beginning to sniffle.

"Talk to Peabody. He can determine your fate," said Cronin. "And Peabody ain't talking. Peabody, where do you get the dope from, if not her? You want to cut her loose?"

"If I did tell you who I got the stuff from, what would you do?" said Peabody.

"I'd try and catch'em," said Cronin.

"I could tell you it was Joe Blow," said Peabody.

"You ain't going to tell me it is Joe Blow and I ain't going to accept that," said Cronin.

"You come at a bad time, Mr. Cronie."

"Listen," said Cronin. "We're not saying you are the French Connection, don't get me wrong. But for every big operation there are thousands of small ones and this is one of them."

"Look," Peabody said, stalling. "People come here cause I got good dope. I buy from a guy named Cuba."

"Cuba what?"

"I don't know no last names."

"Yeah," said Cronin. "Fidel Castro's nephew. You know Peabody, you aren't depressed from being out here in the ghetto. You are depressed from being so dumb and not asking no last names. Do you think the three of us just started working on the street last night?"

"Don't be mad, Mr. Cronie. Peabody! Don't make him mad," begged the girl. "I only come here to borrow $10."

The policemen gathered up the bags of heroin and led the two out of the garage. They waited while Peabody padlocked the place up. Then they climbed in the squad car which had been brought around to the garage door a few minutes earlier and started to slowly roll down the alley, lights still off. From out of one of the backyards, the figure of a man appeared. He went furtively to the garage door and knocked three times.

"Another fucking customer," said one of the cops.

"Marshall Fields should be so lucky," said Cronin and they headed for the station.

"THE MURDER BUILDING:
"NOTHING GOOD HAPPENS THERE."

Standing motionless in the dark hallway, Cronin could hear footsteps upstairs. And a woman whispering in some corner of a stairwell. And the low rasp of some male voices making a drug deal.

He flicked on his flashlight and walked on into the hollow hall of a dark derelict apartment building, past apartments that looked as if a battle had been fought there, room to room, until there was nothing left to destroy or defend and then moved on. A December wind blew in through the vacant windows and tattered window shades twisted and banged in wild response like broken sails on a ghost ship -- knock, knock, knocking against the sills. The hall floor was rotted, soggy from a lake of water tumbling from a broken pipe that once led to a toilet, long since ripped out and hauled away.

He got to a door that was closed and put his ear to it. Inside, he could hear muffled human sounds. He knocked. When there was no answer, he pushed it open. The light of a TV set and a space heater illuminated the room where three children lay on a urine streaked mattress. Two of the children, both girls, appeared to be asleep. The third, and the oldest, a boy about 7 or 8, stared at Cronin with large brown eyes. Except for a small area, about five feet by three feet, between the door and the old mattress, the room was not negotiable. It was filled with hand me down clothes, soaking wet and mildewing in piles up to four feet high. They were mixed in with discarded shoes, a bicycle frame, two stained lamp shades, and a Mickey Mouse book bag. Next to the bed was a bucket filled with plastic plates crusted with old food. The room reeked of urine and cockroaches, hundreds of them, moved in wild herds, across the walls.

A woman, pipe thin, came out of what must have once been the bathroom.

"I thought you were moving," said Cronin, to the squatter woman.

"I was, officer, but the truck ain't come to move my furniture."

"This stuff shouldn't be moved, it should be burned," said Cronin. He turned and saw that behind him a man was sitting on the remains of a chair. He had not noticed him when he walked in for he was leaning against the entrance wall. The man's hands were hanging limply at his sides and his head was bowed down, hanging loosely from his neck.

"You still here too?" asked Cronin.

The man couldn't lift his head; it was stone heavy from a drug stupor. He nodded once but could not speak. This was the second time Cronin had found the woman, her man and the three kids squatting here.

The first time, a week before, she and he, along with three other men, were smoking cocaine and sitting in a slow motion haze while the children lay on the mattress, ignored but watching. She had disposed of the drugs in the bathroom that night just as she probably had done tonight when she heard Cronin at the door.

"I thought I told you to leave last week. You said you were going," said Cronin. "I want these kids out of here. There's no heat here. This is no way for a kid to live. Are you listening? This building is condemned. It's supposed to be empty. It's illegal to be here."

"I know," said the woman, limply, "but I ain't got no other place to go. I be paying rent from my welfare check to another apartment but the truck ain't come yet for my stuff and I ain't got no more money."

"You found the money to be buying cocaine, didn't you?" said Cronin. He looked down at the oldest child who was watching him.

"Do you go to school?" he asked the boy.

The boy nodded a half-yes.

"Where?"

The boy shrugged. He didn't know the name.

""How old are you?"

"Eight."

"What grade are you in?"

The boy looked around for an answer. Getting none, he guessed. "Kindergarten?" he said.

"How old is your sister?"

The boy fumbled around with his fingers and held up five.

"Does she go to school?"

The boy looked at his mother and then nodded yes.

"Then she should be in kindergarten, not you," said Cronin.

The boy looked at him blankly.

Cronin looked around, shook his head, and then focused his light down to thread his way back through the clutter to the door without tripping. "Don't be here when I come back," he said.

"I be moving next week," the woman said, anxious to close the door tight once he stepped out. "You can see I got all my stuff packed..."

"I noticed," said Cronin, stepping into the hall and heading for the stairs to the upper floors. Just then two figures were coming down the hall from outside. Cronin flicked off his flashlight and stood to the side, waiting.

When they reached within ten feet of him, he stepped forward and shone his light. It was a man and a woman.

"So what are we doing in here tonight, my man?" said Cronin.

"We're meeting friends," said the woman, thinking fast.

"Oh bullshit. You are here to cop some dope," said Cronin.

"Well, quite honestly, officer. We was looking for that...."

"This place is supposed to be empty...who's selling from here?" asked Cronin.

"Who's selling?" said the man. "Everybody!"

"This ain't the place to be coming," said Cronin. "You know what this building is..."

"I know. I lived here last January," said the woman. "One day I opened my door and there was a body lying right there in front of it. He looked to be about 17 and he had on a mask, like the Lone Ranger, but he was dead."

"So you know better. The two of you, outta here. Business hours are over."

"Yes sir," said the man and the two headed back down the dark hallway. They began arguing and Cronin could hear the woman saying, "I told you about this place. I told you I didn't want to come in here. I told you it ain't safe...everybody know but you...this is the Murder Building."

Cronin had been hearing about the Murder Building for a while now. People on the street had been talking about it. "I be living two blocks from the Murder Building," a kid would say to Cronin when he was asking for his ID. Or, "My girl friend got robbed over in the Murder Building when she went to cop some 'caine," they'd tell him.

"There's a spot for you, Cronie," a junkie told him. Over on Parkside. The Murder Building. Weasel be running drugs out of there but it ain't safe. They be killin's in there."

The Murder Building stood like a crypt, dark and monolithic in the night, at the southwest corner of Parkside and West End. Its windows were smashed out and the frames busted up...like swollen eyes blackened in a fight. Its front lobby door was wide open and hanging from the hinges. Rats skittered and squeaked through its bowels and darted down the black holes of the building, as if they, too, were afraid and didn't want to spend the night. Mud-frozen lots, vacant and desolate of tree or bush, shouldered both sides of it, as if nothing could grow near its deadliness.

It had been abandoned by its owners, forgotten by city inspectors, and lost in the bureaucracy of housing court. The taxes hadn't been paid on it for over 12 years. Fines imposed on the landlord for hundreds of building code violations were ignored. Each time the fines came down, the building just changed landlords.

The three storied 41 unit building had become a monument to the urban slum. And a walk through it, a visit to the Fourth World--which exists only in urban America – that world of tragic contradictions. Where there are free schools but the kids don't go. Where people live in filth and squalor amidst electricity, TV sets and princess phones. Where wads of $100 bills end up in the back pockets of teenagers working dope spots instead of to fix the plumbing or help their mother pay the rent. Where apartments have stoves but nobody cooks--they buy fast food and don't eat together. Where things are broken and not repaired. Where people receive checks but have no checking accounts. Where gangs have replaced family. Where dependency has replaced slavery. Where being "30" is considered old and where few know or must listen to anyone over 50. Where babies are what a man wants to sire, but not what he wants to raise. Where 'tomorrow' is as far away as ten years.

It is a world without direction. Without focus. Without memory or history. Because it is the world Cronin works in it has become part of his world too. And the Murder Building had become the epitome of it, the microcosm of this Fourth World where people entered only to do harm to themselves or someone else.

The Murder Building was an open lair with dungeon-like halls where drug dealers, junkies, robbers and rapists, either clung to its darkness like bats or hid in its paint-peeled rooms, or squatted on disemboweled sofas to smoke cocaine or defecated in the foul smelling bath tubs or roamed the halls looking for a victim.

And there were plenty. In less than one year, there had been 80 criminal incidents – rapes, robberies, and batteries – that police even knew about. There also had been five homicides.

The people on the street knew what they were talking about when they called it the Murder Building.

I stay away from the place," a teen age boy told Cronin as he was standing on a corner a block away. "People be known to go into that building and not come out. Nothing good happens there."

Cronin went there because nobody else did. He didn't go in response to a crime, like the police beat cars. He went there on his own, because that's where crime was happening. And no matter what time of day or night he entered, he found someone hidden somewhere, someone who didn't get out in time or couldn't. If he came in through the front door, cries of "Cronin" would ring out by those who'd spotted him. Deep inside would be the rustle through garbage and the creak of a sill as unseen figures jumped out the windows and ran from him.

One December night, he paid the place another visit. He pulled the squad up the alley and parked it across from what had been its back entrance. The back door was nailed shut and its door handle stolen. The back porch stairs hung precariously and creaking overhead, dangling unconnected to the ground from the second floor. The bottom half had been ripped away.

Instead of climbing up five feet through a back window, he walked around to the front and came in through the crippled front door.

It was being propped open by a Weber grill, which was missing one leg. It was filled with char and on the floor around it were discarded hypodermic needles. The lobby was an obstacle course of partly burned mattresses, overturned sinks, used condoms, empty cans, half pint bottles, and discarded underpants. If they were selling dope upstairs, they'd probably heard him as he stumbled on this garbage in the blackness and would be gone before he made it to the second or third floors.

He was standing there in the dark, listening, when a couple walked in off the street and nearly knocked him over.

"What you doing here, pal. Miss the bus?" asked Cronin. "Uh, no," said the startled man. He had his right arm around a young girl, a teenager with no front teeth and six red barrettes in her bangs. In his left hand, the man held a bottle in a brown bag. He and she smelled of gin.

"Really, officer. I just come in here to get laid," said the man.

"This ain't a whore house, it's a Murder House," said Cronin.

"Then we're leaving right now," the man said and hustled the girl out with him.

Cronin could hear no foot traffic upstairs. No whispers in a stairwell. No sounds of a drug deal going down. But way down the hall, up over a mountain of trash, as if bulldozed there to be an obstacle, he could see a crack of light coming out from under a closed door.

"Not someone else living here," said Cronin and he climbed up the mountain of trash, slid down, maneuvered around an old bath tub and squished his way down the water-soaked hall. He knocked on the door. It opened a crack.

"Po-lice," said Cronin and pushed the door open wide. A small effeminate man wearing three sweaters and a filthy parka backed off to give him entrance space and then stood looking at him. The place was filled with trash, climbing up the walls into peaks and spilling down into foothills. There was no bed amidst the turmoil of garbage, just a sofa with a broken back. The man was a 'he-she', he told Cronin, and worked the streets dressed like a girl.

"I'm a male prostitute," he told Cronin."I work Madison Street."

"You here alone?," asked Cronin.

The male prostitute leaned down and curled up on the broken sofa, recoiled into a small ball, and pulled a filthy blanket up over him. He was cold. When he did so, it exposed a small brown dog with big ears who'd been taking a nap there. On the floor, by his head, nested in old rags, was a cat who had just had kittens.

"No," said the man, pointing at the animals. "I live here with them. My good friends."

"What the hell are you doing here?"asked Cronin.

"Don't got no other place to go," he said.

"And you chose this place?" asked Cronin, looking around at the room.

"I know. I lived here once before," said the man, pulling the blanket up to his neck and in doing so, the dog snuggled up closer to his legs. The mother cat was purring despite the dank cold.

"I found a dead person in the hall here once and another outside the front door. When I tell people I live at 146 N. Parkside everyone say, 'Oh, you live in the Murder Building'. I say I know but I just ain't got no place else to go."

"Oh shit," said Cronin. "Look, I'm not going to bother you. But you got to get out of here. You know where you're at. It's called nowhere."

"I know that," said the man. "But I'm not nowhere alone. I got my friends."

Cronin left the small man and walked out. No arrests in the building this night. Just a nightly check. He lumbered out through the unhinged front door and looked down the street for any drug dealing before he turned and started crossing the frozen mud toward the spot where his squad car was parked.

"Tell me there is hope out here," he said more to himself than anyone. "Tell that man there is hope."

As he was walking across the lot toward the alley he looked back and saw a dim light in one window, filtering pale brown through old newspaper taped to glass, shining out from the room he had just left.

Then it suddenly flicked out.

Cronin pulled the car keys from his pocket.

"All is well," Cronin muttered. "Our man and his friends are turning in for the night."

"There are always cop stories told at cop bars and his name always comes up. I've won two medals from the department for heroism but I'd give them up tomorrow if I could be talked about by my peers the way they talk about Mike Cronin."

– Former Police Sergeant Gary Morris

"BEING HERE" IS WHAT DOES IT

"God, I hate this place," said Bobby Drozd getting out of the car and scowling at the two flat on Hubbard Street. They'd been there many times before. It was a smoke house. "I hate it," he said again. "It's always the same."

He and Cronin walked around to the front door and Cronin knocked, in usual fashion, with the butt of his flash light. The people inside knew that knock. It meant Cronin. They always opened but sometimes they took their time, in case they had to dispose of something he shouldn't find. It was 9:30 at night.

A woman answered the door dressed in a robe.

"How you do'in Cronin?" she said without passion. "There ain't no problem here, is there?" She always acted surprised to see the police, as if nothing was ever happening in her house, so why stop by. She left the door open and wandered back into her living room, expecting him and Drozd to follow, which they did. A light colored sofa, and two chairs in the front room were covered with see-through plastic and the woman's husband, dressed only in his undershorts, was sitting watching TV and saying nothing. Cronin and Drozd stood in the living room a minute and talked to her about some gang members, her children's age, who'd been coming around to her house.

"I don't want to see them no more," she said. That, Cronin didn't believe.

Cronin looked straight back through the living to the dining room and the kitchen, a route heavily traveled for the rug was worn thin in a path that led to a basement door in the kitchen. Next to the basement door was a large kitchen closet, its door open and legs sticking out of it. As Cronin approached and looked in, he saw it was a person, his top half inside the closet, his lower half sticking out, either sleeping or passed out. Nobody in this first floor apartment paid any attention to the comatose figure nor gave an excuse for it. Cronin walked around the protruding legs, still wearing its gym shoes, opened the basement door and descended the circular stairs.

He reached the basement landing and was greeted by thick blue smoke, six faces pretending they hadn't heard him come down the steps, sitting around a table laden with glass smoking pipes, still hot to the touch but nothing left in them. The place was as sullen as a Chinese opium den.

Nobody said a word nor made a move, except a big lanky man named General who flicked the ash off his Kool into a jar lid.

"Are we having a birthday party? You're having so much fun," said Cronin. "You must be. And these must be the party favors," he said, taking his flash light and smashing the pipes into tiny shards. "Now, who is the birthday boy?"

Drozd had turned in another direction. Cronin had gone right at the bottom of the stairs, to the live participants around the table. Drozd went left into the recovery room, still saying to himself, "I hate this place." He pulled back a grubby blanket hanging as a divider over a clothes line that had been strung up. Behind it was a large room next to the furnace filled with old re-cycled couches and comatose figures sprawled out on each one. Drozd circled his flash light around the room looking at each human lying there, wrapped in raggedy blankets and drooling, so stoned they couldn't even snore. He leaned over and tried to rouse one but the man didn't even grunt. The oblivion he'd sought through cocaine had been found.

Cronin was searching the group at the table. Asking them their names and ages. All of them looked older than the age they gave. One of them, a youth in his twenties, Cronin recognized before he gave his name. His name was Brian and he was wanted on a subpoena regarding the murder of a young girl. Brian was a witness. He told Cronin he didn't care about the death of the girl, he didn't want to go into the station.

"A little girl got murdered and you are going in with me--I don't care what you want," said Cronin. Drozd joined Cronin and searched General, looking in his pants pockets, in his shirt pockets and then, inside his hat. Tucked carefully in the inside hat band was a gram of cocaine.

"The birthday boy," said Drozd.

"You been to the joint," said Cronin.

"Yeah," said General.

"You on parole?" said Cronin.

"Yeah," said General, tightening the muscles in his face until they were taught, as if he were about to cry.

"Then you got to go too."

Drozd led the two, General and Brian, who complained all the way out to the squad car. Drozd would talk to them in the back seat.

Cronin came up from the basement to the first floor--gave a mere nod to the lady and man of the house who were still studiously watching TV on their plastic covers-- and then at the vestibule, ascended the stairs to the second floor apartment. They knew him up there too.

"Who is it?" said a light female voice.

"Cronin," he answered.

"Oh, it's you," the voice said and the door opened. An attractive young black woman stood there and said, "Come on in." Her last name was Love.

She led him into her kitchen which was homey and well scrubbed. Over at the table five small children were playing with dolls and coloring books. She introduced them to Cronin and they all looked up and smiled. The two youngest ran over and hugged his legs. She returned to the board where she'd been ironing and tested the back of the iron with a wetted finger and it steamed. She started working on a shirt collar and looked up at Cronin, friendly and ready to talk. Her husband, a gang member, was in prison. She lived there with her children, her sister, TuTu, and her sister's children. Her sister's husband, a gang member and drug dealer whom Cronin had arrested scores of times, had recently been executed by hit men for holding up their drug spots. Her sister, in her early twenties, was already a widow. It was a house filled with children and no man around.

She and Cronin talked about what was new on the streets. Who was in prison, who was awaiting prison, who was dead, and who was running things in certain neighborhoods.

"You've got some nice kids here," said Cronin. "How can you be living here knowing what is going on downstairs and in the basement?"

"I know Cronie," said the woman, looking up from the shirt she was ironing. "You always warned us, don't shit where we eat."

"Somebody could get shot in this place. One of the kids could get hurt...they could go down there and see that shit..."

"I know, Cronie. You're right."

"Then get them out of here. How many people are passing through here each day?" he asked.

"Fifteen to twenty," she said.

"No, more like forty to fifty," said Cronin.

"Not anymore, Cronin. It's slowing down in the basement. And me and my sister is getting out of here."

"We'll see. Nothing is slowing down out here," he said.

Cronin and the woman made their good-bys. Drozd and the two prisoners were waiting for him in the car.

"That one building tells the story of the West Side," said Cronin later. "Upstairs, on the second floor, you have five little kids, innocent and clean, cutting out paper dolls. On the first floor you have a family where all the kids have joined gangs and the mother and father knowingly rent out the basement to whoever pays to get in. Then down in the basement you got the bust out junkies, smoking and passing out.

"Now what chance do those kids on the second floor have? Will those kids go from the second floor and end up in the basement? Tell me. How long? Out here these kids don't go bad, they never have a chance to go good."

Drozd was in the car, repeating Cronin's words, when Cronin climbed in.

"This goes on every day. There's places like this all over the West Side. I hate coming here....I hate that basement."

In the back seat, Brian, high on cocaine, began to bang his head against the window of the car.

"I ain't got nothing to say about no murder," he said.

"Watch out," said Drozd, turning and looking at him. "You keep banging your head, you might knock some sense into it. Then what would you do, huh?"

"I wouldn't be sitting in the back of no squad," said Brian.

"The hell you wouldn't," said Drozd. "Smarts don't break a habit."

General was crying and not bothering to wipe away his tears.

"I'm on parole. You know what that means, Cronie. I got to go back to prison...I'm going back, Oh God, I got to go back!"

"You had it on you." said Cronin. "We got to lock ya up."

"You just get out?" asked Drozd.

"Just got out," said General.

"You were in the program for a year while you were in prison, right?" said Cronin.

"Yeah, for a year."

"Then how'd you get right back on it?" said Cronin. "C'mon. Be honest, man."

"I'm being honest, Cronie," said General. "It's being here. You know what the west side can do. It's just being here."

POST SCRIPT: Brian never testified in the murder of the young girl. He refused to. He was later charged with murder in another case. General was sent back to prison for another two years, "probably saving him from dying for a little bit longer," said Cronin. And several months later, Love's brother was let out of prison. He was shot and killed in that basement on Hubbard Street. The lady in the robe and the man in the undershorts who sat on plastic and watched TV on the first floor were his parents. Although it happened in his own home, it was ruled justifiable homicide for he was pulling out a gun when he got shot. It's not clear whether the five children upstairs on the second floor heard the shot or saw the body of their uncle lying dead down below.

KENNY, THE HARD-WORKING TEACUP MAN

Kenny wasn't a lazy kid. In fact, he was a hard worker for a 17 year old. He found a full time job the day after he got out of St. Charles, the jail for juveniles west of Chicago. And he'd only been out two weeks. Twice in the last week, Cronin had seen him in the lobby of the Washington Pines Hotel when he walked in, looking nonchalant while everyone else who had been hanging around beat feet the minute they saw Cronin's squad car passing outside the lobby window. Except for a man in a wheel chair, who couldn't run, and the lady behind the desk who didn't need to, Kenny would be the only one still standing in the shabby lobby.

This time, after everyone ran, Cronin invited Kenny out into the back seat of his squad car. He was going to name check him. As usual, he drove him away from the hotel, parked somewhere dark, and cut the headlights.

"So what the fuck are you doing there?" asked Cronin.

"Working," said Kenny. "It's a straight up job...I make $250 a week."

"Two fifty doing what?....working as a lookout for all the drug dealers in that shit hole hotel?" said Cronin. "You call that straight up?"

"Yeah but I go to work everyday, Cronin. I work 8 hours a day, seven days a week, the 4 p.m. to midnight shift. For real. I ain't missed a day."

"How come everyone was running when I came in?" asked Cronin, as if he didn't know.

"They saw you riding," said Kenny.

"Well, what happens when I come in?"

"We'll get out before you get in," said Kenny

"There are a couple of dope spots upstairs in the apartments. How much they keep in one spot?"

"A G-ball ($1000 worth)."

"Who's dope is it?" asked Cronin.

"Ice Mike's."

"How do you get it, when are you re-supplied?"

"We beep when we need it and someone come to the hotel and bring it up. They got a lookout here for you, Cronin. Everybody get tipped off the minute they see you drive by."

"So when I come in, what happens?" said Cronin.

"Unless you got a search warrant, they okay in the apartments where they selling. They figure ya don't know which ones, 'cause they change. But to be safe, they give the bags to some guys like me and we go to the elevators and we take one, stop it between floors and turn the lights off while the police is searching all over. And if they think we are in there, we drop the dope down the elevator shaft and get out with nothing on us. We clean. The po-lice never search down there at the bottom of the elevator and we pick it up later. And the cops leave cause they ain't found nothing."

"You're going to get caught," said Cronin. "I know you're a look-out..."

"If I started selling for them, I could be making more--$550 week," said Kenny.

"I'm saying you're going to get caught. And I'm going to try to catch you. You just got out of St. Charles, ya goof. You are an adult now. You're seventeen. The next time it ain't going to be no kiddy home for naughty boys. Why are ya doing this?"

"I need work, Cronie," said the kid.

"Why don't ya go home?" said Cronin."You're not from over here."

"Ain't nothing at home," said the boy. "There ain't nothing to go home to." The kid was empty.

"Ya want to get out here?" said Cronin ending the conversation, "or do you want me drop you off somewhere else?"

"Sure, this okay," said Kenny, preparing to open the door and get out.

"Remember, you're 17. St. Charles is a thing of the past. You are in the big leagues now. You're not wearing short pants anymore. And if you're dirty, I'm going to get ya."

"I hear ya, Cronin," said the kid. And he ambled back toward the hotel.

A month later, Cronin got a tip on a building the people on the street called the Tea Cup place. It was just a block down Pine Street from the hotel where Kenny worked. It was a fifties style blond-brick apartment building, two stories high. Day and night, there was a lookout sitting in a kitchen chair on the public sidewalk at the entrance to the side gangway. The lookout wore a whistle on a string around his neck. It was usually an older man, who looked innocent enough, like he was out breathing in the evening air. His wife often came out to talk to him.

Cronin scouted the place out and saw the first floor rear apartment was empty. The next evening, once it was dark, he and an officer named McGuire came down the alley, climbed the back fence and went in through a half open window to the rear first-floor apartment. They could not have come through the door if they'd wanted, for it was barricaded with a metal bar and only the right word with the right face would have gotten it to open. Cronin did not have the right face.

Cronin and McGuire sat in silence in the dark of the empty apartment waiting and listening. But not for long. They heard a whistle coming from the street and then the window up above them opened. A hand protruded from the upstairs window holding the shard from a broken mirror. Not having to show his face by peering out, whoever was upstairs could see who had passed the whistling lookout and was approaching down the gang way to make an order. The customer was sized up before he got there. Then he stood directly in front of the first floor window where Cronin and McGuire were hiding and shouted up his order to the second floor. Quickly a tea cup was lowered down on a string.

"Four dime bags," the customer said and he placed four ten dollar bills in the tea cup.

117

Up went the tea cup banging against the bricks, as if it were rising toward Rapunzel in her tower, and then down it came again, four sealed plastic bags of cocaine in the tea cup. The customer grabbed his purchase and left quickly by the back gate. And up went the tea cup.

Cronin and McGuire watched it happen twice and then they'd seen enough. They left the first floor apartment, went upstairs from the inside, knocked on the door and when it was answered, Cronin saw a familiar face, working hard, still employed seven days a week, but making more money. It was Kenny. He was no longer a look-out, he'd become the Tea Cup man.

"Ya fucking goof," said Cronin while he was arresting him. "You're in the big leagues now."

"I know, Cronie," said the boy. "But it's what I've been doing for a long time."

"The hell it is," said Cronin. "You're only seventeen."

"But Cronin," he said, looking him straight in the eye."

"I been doing this since I was ten."

"BUT YOU DIDN'T STOP THE DEALING"

During the night, a great thunderstorm rolled in from the West, one of those wonderful phenomena of the American prairie, rumbling over the flats of the city sounding like war drums from a Roman legion and crackling electric blue light that arched the sky trying to mate the clouds. The storm's water poured down straight and hard and battered the roofs of the West Side. The street gutters, already cluttered with trash, backed-up and made tiny lakes which melded with the ponds in the pot holes. The rain beat the sidewalks clean and tiny waterfalls curled over the broken curbs and rinsed them of flotsam. The storm was a godsend, hosing down the grime filled, tired city for a new and sunlit weekend.

By late morning, after nature's army had marched on toward the East, grumbling a warning as it left, the air was thick and smelled of green and black dirt. In back yards, dandelions arched up an inch higher and it looked as if someone during the night had tossed golden coins into spots where grass would not grow. Queen Anne's Lace uncurled its delicate blooms, turning abandoned lots into sudden meadows of whispering white.

It was on this ripe late afternoon in May, Cronin decided to go to Rockwell Gardens, a public housing project just off the Eisenhower expressway at Western Avenue. This was the housing project that Jack Kemp, Secretary of Housing and Urban Development had just visited two months earlier and, with much press coverage and ballyhoo, praised the city and the Chicago Housing Authority for their attempts to restore order in public housing buildings.

At 117 S. Rockwell, a high rise building within the Rockwell Gardens Complex, there had been no attempt to restore anything and there was no order. The only outsiders who ventured in there regularly were the police, the fire department paramedics and customers to the drug trade.

No pizza delivery man, no florist, no newspaper boy would even try. No Sears trucks pulled up. No piano teacher stopped in to give lessons. No dry cleaners dropped off the clothes. The paramedics and the police were often targets if not of overt violence, then of antagonism. But the customers for drugs generally walked in and out untouched, protected by the muscle of the drug dealers. If they got mugged, robbed, hassled or their cars broken into while they were making their buy, there would soon be no customers. No customers, no business. No business, no money. No money for anybody. And so, if the customers stuck to the first floor, and did not invite ambush by going into the stairwells or elevators, they could make their buy and leave having ventured successfully into the very corridors that many of the building's own tenants feared at night. It was like stopping for a hot dog or running into K-Mart on an errand.

Business, at 117 S. Rockwell, therefore, was on the first floor and active. It was a bull market. There were two red plastic milk crates set upside down at the east end of the first floor breezeway and it was from those two crates that the dealers set up shop, like a POP stand – except their pop was spelled PCP. Those two crates were inviolate. It was understood they were not to be moved. They marked the spot. Even toddlers didn't try to climb on them during the morning hours when business was down and no one was there. They, or the mothers, knew better. This was the PCP building.

Other buildings in the complex had heroin, cocaine, or reefer. But 117 S. Rockwell had PCP, the animal tranquillizer; the stuff that makes you crazy.

It had only been two months earlier that Cronin made an arrest farther west, catching a man in his twenties with heroin on him. He had a bad habit and he had just made a buy. He had a job, he told Cronin. He was involved with the Midnight League, a league of basketball teams from the Chicago public housing complexes. The idea came from Vince Lane, the head of the Chicago Housing

Authority, whose sole purpose in organizing and funding the teams was to lure young men off the streets and away from drugs into a sport they all loved--basketball. To guarantee they would not be out at the most violent and tempting hours, the games were played at midnight. This man was one of their coaches. He was from Rockwell Gardens and some of his family members had sold drugs there for years. He obviously had not kicked the habit, for as he talked to Cronin after his arrest, he was visibly getting sick and starting to sweat. Cronin bought him two candy bars to tide him over before he was I-bonded out. The coach was probably released from lock-up and back in Rockwell Gardens before Cronin finished correcting the misspelled words on his arrest report.

It was this pervasive use and acceptance of drugs that the police were fighting in the projects and not very successfully. For the buildings were wide open, the private CHA security guards were either never around or part of the whole conspiracy. Although the Chicago police would roar up in their cars and come running into the buildings, trying to actually catch anyone with drugs was a real cat and mouse game. The project buildings were citadels--immune to surprise.

"How do we fight this?" Cronin's captain used to grumble over at Gang Crimes West headquarters. "They have an amazing lookout system in all directions. Going in there to end this drug dealing is like trying to catch someone who has disappeared into the catacombs."

"If anyone tells you we are winning this war, tell them they are wrong," said Cronin as he drove up to 117 S. Rockwell this warm and humid evening. "Because we're not. And we won't tonight either. I just want to watch what really goes on when they don't think I'm there."

He banged the squad door closed and gingerly stepped over a large pot hole still filled with the storm water from the night before. He was with three other policemen and tonight they didn't run, they walked in. Past the ladies out bar-b-queing for the evening supper, past tribes of little children skipping rope and bouncing off each other. The smaller ones all stopped and stared. One of the littlest stepped forward and asked, "Is you the po-lice?"

"That we are," said Cronin.

Young teenagers, who only grow in clumps, pretended not to notice as they passed. The police went in and looked around the first floor breezeway.

"What a surprise," said Cronin, looking at the two vacant red milk crates in the hall. "Nobody is sitting on the thrones. Nobody holding court. Where is everybody?"

He turned to a young boy who was trailing close behind him watching him curiously.

"Where do you think everyone went?" he asked the boy. The boy appeared to be about 14 and slightly retarded.

"They all upped and ran when they saw you coming," said the boy.

The four policemen then separated and went different ways, one down the hall, one up the stairs, one into the elevator. The lookouts and a hundred other pairs of eyes couldn't keep track. When two of them walked out later, one at a time, and not together, nobody knew which cop was where or if they now were all gone. Grapes and Baby Face left. But a third was still on an upper floor and Cronin had ducked into an empty apartment at the far east end of the first floor breezeway.

The door handle had been stolen and left in its absence was a round circular two inch peep hole in the wooden door that looked directly out to the two upside down red milk crates. They were only ten feet away.

"They gone," came a shout as one of the lookouts watched Grapes and Baby Face's squad round the corner by the tracks and disappear. Within thirty seconds, the first floor hall became alive....the lookouts back at their posts. The sellers back on their thrones. Cronin watched it all through the peep hole. The guy sitting on the right hand crate was the money man. The customer paid him first. Then the man sitting on the left hand crate, who held the PCP, handed over the merchandise. Action around the crates became intense...a crowd had gathered..as close and clustered and intense, with as archaic hand signals and as shrill of voice, as any group of traders on the floor of the Mercantile Exchange.

"One coming back," shouted a lookout from the west. "Two coming back," shouted another from the north. Business was hopping. Small girls were skipping rope just meters from where they were selling. Three women, not blinking an eye in their direction, wandered down and posted a sign for a meeting of welfare mothers the following Tuesday. A well padded woman with heavy thighs and flip-flops on her swollen feet waddled by, both hands holding grocery bags. She was being trailed by three grandchildren who followed her single-file like ducklings. A CHA janitor for the building came over to the drug dealers, slapped their hands and started jiving in between buys. Dealing drugs didn't bother him at all.

The most active look-out kept calling from the west. Cronin learned later he was only 13. He shouted back every minute with the enthusiasm of the "Caall for Philllipp Moorris!" boy, his young soprano voice rising above the baritones of the older men.

After twenty five transactions, Cronin had enough. He talked quietly on his radio to the policeman upstairs. He described the man holding the drugs. Cronin would come through the door as his partner came up from behind. Except while they were talking, one of the lookouts decided he wanted to relieve himself and, as finding a toilet would be too time consuming, he walked to the door of the empty apartment just ten feet away where Cronin was hiding, pushed it open with one hand and began unzipping his pants with the other. He found little relief for he banged smack into Cronin who was barging out. The commotion set them off in the breezeway like frightened birds. The cop from upstairs was on his way toward them but the element of surprise was gone. The man with the drugs dropped a gun he had in his hand and ran. But he kept the PCP cradled somewhere on his body for he would have to answer financially for that loss.

The money man got caught before he could split. He dropped the money on the floor but didn't run fast enough. He had a gun on him and he was on parole for murder. He was arrested.

"I know I'm going back to the joint," he said, resigned. And so he talked. The first floor hall where the two red thrones were located was rented from the street gang that controlled the building for $500 a day--basically from 9 a.m. until midnight. The gang member they paid lived on the ninth floor. But it was worth it because in a good 15 hour shift, you could sell $6,000 worth of PCP.

Every morning, four of the younger boys were picked to work as lookouts for $100 a day --one for each direction of the winds. They had to be young and attentive or they wouldn't be hired back the following day. Most importantly, they had to be fleet of foot--able to outrun even the longest legged cop.

"You assholes were dealing like crazy," Cronin said to his prisoner back in the station. "Doing it in front of the women, the grandmothers and the kids. The fucking janitor. And nobody beefs...I don't get it."

"That's cause we ain't selling to no kids, Cronie," said the man.

"Kids? You have 13-year-olds working as looks outs, what do you consider a kid?"

"We don't sell drugs to no kids," the man insisted. "If he's a boy and wearing shorts, he's too young. If she's girl and wearing a skirt, she old enough to buy."

"Ain't that a bitch," said Cronin, rolling the arrest form into a typewriter that was as old as he.

"You know, they got a replacement for me already, probably sitting on the crate, taking in the money over there," said the man.

"As we speak, I'm sure," said Cronin, not looking up.

The prisoner leaned back in his chair and adjusted his right arm which was handcuffed, in Cronin fashion, to the office door knob.

"Ya stopped me Cronin, but ya didn't stop the dealing," he said.

"You're right," said Cronin, looking up over his half glasses from Osco's. "You know, I just do what I got to do. I'm not God. I'm only man."

"I hear ya, Cronin," said the prisoner with a knowing smile. "Me too!"

THE NIGHT LUTHER DIDN'T
KNOW HER NAME

God, she didn't think they saw her. Oh Jesus! They didn't really see her, did they? Not at the distance this squad car was coming in from. They couldn't have seen her put the dope in her purse. Could they? Oh Jesus! And she'd just walked out the door. Luther had passed it into her hand at the curb of the parking lot. She didn't know why then – but she knew now. Because he saw what was coming. The cops.

They were supposed to be off by now; everyone knew that. But there they were after 1:30 a.m.--their quitting time--and they drove their squad car banging and clanking over the pot holes and piles of unbagged garbage up to within four feet of where she was standing, their headlights directly on her, blinding her eyes and making her squint. They knew. They saw it. Oh Jesus! She knew they knew.

They were out of the car before the engine was silent, leaving their doors open and they walked straight up to her. They asked her to open her purse. And then, when she did, fumbling at the clasps which weren't even closed because she'd done it all in such a hurry, they found the bags of dope sticking out. They turned to Luther, the man she loved that night, and asked him why he did that--passed her the dope. And she was protesting, saying it wasn't hers or his or anybody else's, matter of fact, as she was being hauled off to the back of the squad car.

She heard Luther say to Cronin, "I don't know that bitch. Don't even know her name."

And then she cried. It started off with silent tears and whispers to God while she was in the back seat. Almighty Jesus! Oh God! Almighty Jesus! And then she began shrieking as they got closer to the station and she began banging her head against the back window.

From the front seat, in chorus and without turning around, because they'd heard it a thousand times before, Cronin and Drozd told her, "Shut up." They said it with finality. And she did. She settled into a practiced whimper and kept it up all the way to Area 4 headquarters, through the back door as they walked in and down the corridor into their office. They ignored it.

The door closed, Cronin sat down at the typewriter, adjusted his half glasses, and poised himself to write the arrest report. Drozd went into another room to weigh the dope. She composed herself six feet away from them on a metal chair and drew in a few deep breaths.

"Okay, your name, last name first and spell it," said Cronin, starting to peck away at a 40 year old typewriter.

"Diane," she said.

"Last name first, and tell me if you have been arrested before," said Cronin.

"Oh, Jesus! Oh God Almighty. Oh Jesus, save me," she said, starting up again. It was his. It wasn't mine. He gave it to me."

"I know," said Cronin, "but it was in your purse."

"I thought he was my man," she said, starting to weep and half slide off the chair in defeat, dropping her purse weakly onto the floor.

"You want to help us do a case on him. You want to testify against him? I'll do it," said Cronin.

She shook her head no.

"Well, you ain't his woman then because he set you up. You took the case for him. Luther is a son of a bitch, you know that, Diane, right? Okay, your birth date?"

"You typing it all up? I'm really being arrested? Save me Jesus," she wailed. "Oh my mama gonna kill me."

"Diane, shut up! How old are you?"

"Twenty seven."

"You'll be out tomorrow ... no, today because it is already tomorrow. It's 2:15 in the morning. You'll be out today, after court. Why don't you stay away from motherfuckers like him?"

"Oh Cronin. I will. I will. I will never see that man again. He gave me up. I don't mean nothing to him. He said he didn't even know me. How can he say that? He know me. He know me a long time. He say he don't even know my name."

Cronin's two index fingers had stopped their pecking on the typewriter and his hands loitered impatiently three inches over the keys. It was getting late. "Your address, Diane?"

"I stay on the north side," she said, and she spelled out the address. Cronin began typing again.

"Well, you go back up to the north side when they release you from court," said Cronin. "Don't be coming around here. I better not see you out there again."

"I won't, Cronie. I promise. I'm on medication, see, and I need to get some more pills up there at a clinic near my house. I ain't going to see that man ever. You'll never see me down here... Say, Cronie, can I use the phone? I need to call my mama. Maybe I'll stop by my mama's house and stay with her. I won't be hanging with Luther no more. Not with no man who say he don't even know my name. I swear."

"Okay, Diane. Here's the phone," said Cronin. "Call your mama."

Diane got up, walked limply over to the desk, dialed a number, leaned against the wall and then said, "Mama, I been arrested. I know mama..." and she started to cry again. "Mama, they say I be out sometime today. I'll be coming by then. Yes, mama. I'll come straight there. I promise."

At 1:30 a.m. the following morning, Cronin and Drozd pulled into the same parking lot in the projects. A crowd was standing there, looking stunned and surprised again by the headlights which were working late. And in the middle of all of them was Luther and next to him ...

"It's fucking Diane," said Cronin, jumping out of the car. "With her man Luther. What you got hidden on you this time, Diane? More of Luther's dope? When did ya...didn't you just get out?"

She tried not to look at him. but it was hard not to. He was right up in her face. About as tall as she was.

127

"What ya got in your hand?" he shouted.

She opened her palm and disclosed a crumpled piece of paper she'd been clutching. It was her bond slip. She'd been released just three hours before from night court.

"You got out three hours ago? What did ya do? Go home to mama? No! Ya took the fucking bus straight back to the man who didn't even know your name. He know your name now? Huh?"

Diane didn't nod yes or no or even answer the question. Her eyes looked far off, searching for another place to be. A place she hadn't found yet. She bit her lip. Luther was slowly moving away.

Disgusted, Cronin turned his back. The lecture was over. His partner, Drozd, had found the dope this time in a baby's diaper. The mother holding the baby was standing right behind Luther.

"Putting it on a baby now, that's sweet Luther," said Cronin. "Just plain fucking sweet." Drozd already had the mother in the back seat; the baby was left behind, crying in the arms of an auntie, and reaching its small hands out for its mother who looked back twice through the window.

The squad backed up and pulled out. The headlights caught a female figure walking off from the crowd, head down, back heaving, stumbling down a small lane that led to Madison Street. There was a bus stop there. The police car turned right. Diane kept walking toward that bus stop and disappeared from sight, sobbing her nightly refrain, "Almighty Jesus. God Save me!"

SIX WOMEN, FOURTEEN KIDS AND HE WASN'T EVEN TRYING

Luther was working on his car...or somebody's car...and he had the hood up, the trunk open, the windows down, the radio on and he was deeply engrossed in something under the hood of an old Lincoln that wasn't working right. And then Cronin pulled up. Luther had found as private a place as possible in the projects to set up shop- -no gangbangers taunting him, no little kids dancing into his way, no security guards bugging him, no ladies to distract him and no shots being fired randomly across the grassless grassy sprawls called DMZ's. Here he didn't have to watch his back while he bent down and listened to what was making the clanking sound. He was on a side street at the very eastern end of the Rockwell Gardens housing projects.

Cronin had known him for years. Luther and his family sold dope. Not big time dope, but a steady income to supplement their welfare checks. It made life comfortable for an easygoing man like Luther.

Cronin hadn't seen Luther for a couple of months--not since that night he and his partner Drozd saw him slipping the dope to Diane.

"You see Diane lately," said Cronin, getting out of the car.

"Nah, ain't seen her in four or five months. She got sent to drug school," said Luther.

"You were a dog putting that case on her," said Cronin.

"Listen, she did it, man. That girl have a mental problem," said Luther, setting a screw driver down on the rear of the Lincoln .

"How could you give a girl like her...it was your dope," said Cronin.

"Listen Cronie, I'm telling you that ain't the way," said Luther.

"The case is over now," said Cronin."I'm not trying to trick you. But I saw you hand it to her. I'm telling you, I saw it."

"She had it when she walked out of the building, though," said Luther.

"Then she gave it to you and you gave it back," said Cronin.

"Then she should never a gave it to me. She know she should'a never gave it to me."

Cronin laughed and shook his head.

"Well, why did she give it to ya?"

"Cause she saw y'all coming," said Luther. "Shit, what am I going to do with it when she saw y'all. I gave it back to her."

"You're a bitch, Luther," said Cronin. "She took the case. But the dope was yours. You won. She lost."

Luther eased himself into the back seat of the squad, looking back through the rear window every few minutes to make sure his car and the parts lying in the street were still there. They talked about who was selling drugs over at Rockwell and who was carrying guns. What apartment doors--outside of his own-- you could knock on and cop some dope. Luther didn't volunteer anything. Cronin asked and Luther answered-- like a poker player, hinting at, but not showing, his hand. They talked about the private security guards in the projects. One fourth, Luther guessed, were gang members themselves and openly used dope on the job.

"So what's this?" asked Cronin, looking at a card that Luther pulled out of his pocket. He'd asked Luther to show him some ID. It was an MCI charge card in the name of Clyde Smith. Except for a welfare green card in his own name, it was the only ID he had. But it looked official.

"Your name ain't Clyde," said Cronin, frowning.

"That's my old lady's son," Luther said.

"I don't believe ya. I believe you are playing on this fucking card," said Cronin.

"I've been with his mother 23 years," said Luther."They gave him two cards and he gave me one. I ain't used it yet.

"Why the last name Smith? You married to her," said Cronin.

"She don't want to marry me," said Luther.

"After 23 years?"

"She says she ain't ready yet," said Luther.

"Well, how many kids do you and she have?" asked Cronin.

"With her I have five," said Luther.

"You mean you got others too?" asked Cronin.

"I got 14."

"And by how many women?"

"Six or seven," said Luther.

"Don't you know?" asked Cronin.

"It's six. I remember," said Luther.

"Ya mean, while you were with Clyde's mother for 23 years, you were having babies with other women?" asked Cronin.

"Well, yeah. But Cronie, I wasn't trying," said Luther.

"You must have been doing something, if not trying," said Cronin."You got a green card. You're on welfare, Luther. Are all your kids on welfare too?"

"No, well their mothers is," said Luther. "Their mothers is on welfare for'em."

"How old is the oldest?" asked Cronin.

"The oldest is sixteen," said Luther. "But I really had 15 kids. My oldest was the girl that got killed some years ago. The girl that got found in an alley, that was my oldest."

"You know, I never heard about that."

"Yeah," said Luther "Someone raped and killed her. Threw her out of the car on 87th Street."

"Did the police solve it? asked Cronin.

"Well, they caught one guy who got 22 years."

"That ain't much for rape and murder," said Cronin. "How old was she?"

"She was young, Cronin. Only 14."

There was a silence for a moment. Cronin handed Luther back the laminated phone charge card.

"Okay," said Cronin, turning the keys on in the squad. "I'm going over to Rockwell Gardens now. I'll see you over there later. We'll talk, right? "

"Huh? I'm not telling nothing, Cronin," said Luther, getting out of the car and then leaning in toward the window. "I ain't going to be standing there when you show up. I ain't doing no dope right now. Got two bucks in my pocket to prove it."

"I'll catch ya if ya do," said Cronin.

"No way," said Luther with a grin. "I'm a family man."

"I know, Luther," said Cronin, putting the car in forward. "I know. Six women, 14 kids and you weren't even trying."

HER HAT TOLD HER SECRET

At dusk – well before the sun shuts down completely and the walkways fade into ominous caverns of dark and shadow, before the ceiling bulbs at the corridor intersections are unscrewed or smashed out, before the shooting begins out the broken windows of abandoned apartments, before the laughter and cries and low talk that go on in hundreds of apartments piled 16 floors high drift out the open windows and meld into the din of boom box music from the street and the tin jabber of a thousand television sets coming from everywhere, before the yelps of drug dealers calling out their orders from hidden recesses start causing a rustle and the whistles of their lookouts in the breezeways penetrate the night – the old people disappear.

It is the hour when the young take over the castle. Emboldened by the blackness of the labyrinthian corridors that circuit through the project's high rises, they run through them with impunity, loiter without fear, and challenge anyone who dares travel a hallway at night. The castle is theirs until the sun rises again when the old, the very young, the weak, and the timid dare venture out while the armed pirates sleep.

It is that way at the Henry Horner Homes on the West Side of Chicago. It has been that way for years and so it was one summer night when Cronin made a stop to look around and see what band was running the castle that night. He was looking for one of them. Cronin went in alone but not unannounced. The lookouts were at their posts and did what they are paid to do. They emitted long low whistles of warning and then faded into the shadows and out of his path. Cronin lumbered in, the radio on his side turned down to a low crackle, a long black metal flash light in his right hand. He walked into a first floor breezeway where the light bulb was dark and only a stubble of glass.

He turned right toward a clump of people standing together, making lots of noise and not worrying about the hour. They stopped it when he walked up. The young men were decked out in the same uniform, new sneakers that came up over their ankles, the laces untied. Their new work-out pants were unzipped from the ankle up far enough to reveal muscular thighs and their hats were all cocked, one way, to the right. The girls wore new stone washed jeans, tight at the ankle, and had beads in their braids. The girls were leaning dolefully against the wall next to the men when Cronin walked up. They stopped giggling and cracking their gum when he appeared out of the dark. A couple of them, barely teenagers, held babies.

"Straighten your hats, man," said Cronin. Quickly, but with gritted teeth, they all did. A few of the young men in the back started to saunter off. The girls turned and started walking nonchalantly back to an apartment door, looking back to see if Cronin was still there and how long they had to be gone from the action.

Cronin started asking for ID's and patting down the men, carrying on a patter of talk with them about their gang generals with nicknames like Nap Dog or Ice Mike, Minister Ed or General Lee --the ones who call it when it comes to running the castle corridors at night.

Up behind them, unnoticed, trudged an old black woman, bent over, scanning for cans and wearing a hat. She had on no new clothes, no above the ankle white gym shoes that fit her bunyoned feet just right or sweat pants fresh from the store that would spare her thick legs from alley scratches or keep her thighs warm at night. Instead, she wore three layers of shirts and skirts and underneath all that, a pair of pants-- a discarded treasure she'd probably found wet and stained in the alley. She had rolled them up above her knees and her black socks stopped at mid calf--drooping a bit at the top because the elastic was stretched. She was wearing a pair of men's shoes that were too big and too wide for her so she stumbled as she walked. She had swollen varicose veins that roiled up her legs and bubbled behind her knees. She had worked hard once and for a long time. She pushed an old baby buggy and kept her eyes to the ground. The young men paid her no heed as she rummaged at their feet.

Word had traveled quickly that Cronin was there and above him, heads peered out the open windows and a piece of trash fell from a window, from somewhere up above. The old woman scurried over to inspect it and see if it belonged in her buggy filled with collectibles. It didn't. It was a whisky bottle and next to it was a soiled baby diaper. She returned to her buggy and pushed unobtrusively toward Cronin and the men. Cronin now was patting them down, asking them to empty their pockets and one casually threw his pop can, half filled, onto the cement floor and it clunked heavily, spilling out brown cola and rolled at the old woman's feet. She ignored it, and pushed her floppy old buggy on past them, body bent over the handle, head down, glancing up for a brief and knowing second at Cronin but giving nothing away. There were deep brown veins that rivered through the whites of her eyes and she nodded ever so slightly at him when she passed.

She stopped and fumbled around with the bulging plastic bags in her beat up baby buggy once she made it by. She fussed around and looked busy as she stood and listened to Cronin tell one of the men, a defiant one with a look of complete boredom on his face, to come with him, he wanted to run a name check--which meant a serious talk in the back seat of the squad car.

"I want you all gone now, outta here, get going, and I fucking mean it," said Cronin, taking the sauntering young pirate with him. Another kid threw down an empty can of pop as he left, swearing to himself about the mother fucking cops. But he and all his buddies dispersed, embarrassed, their maleness threatened by one single cop who was missing a foot. They didn't like someone telling them what to do. Not at night, when they ran the castle, with an old woman watching.

The old woman went back and picked up the pop can. Then stood for a moment, looked around and realized the corridor had fallen silent. It had emptied. Hallelujah! She stood straight up, and smiled. She adjusted her hat which had been pulled down over her

135

white curls and now as she was walking straight, not bending down in fear or groveling in search of garbage, her hat sat pertly on top of her head and you could finally read the inscription above the bill. It said: "I AM A WINNER". She hummed to herself as she and the buggy pushed on. For a brief moment, the castle was hers.

MINNOWS LOST IN THE DEEP

Theirs were the littlest shadows darting down the alley, like tiny playful fish meant for sunlit shallows who dove too deep and found themselves in the darker depths. Minnows amid sharks they were this late night, for it was 1:00 in the morning and no one but predators were out. Unmindful of the deep and the dark shadows they'd ventured into, and, celebrating only their freedom, they careened down alley and gangway, wrestling, and jumping, giggling their way past back yard fences and through abandoned lots. As free as a school of fish. Bouncing off a mattress that lay rotting in a yard, throwing sticks, inspecting old shoes they found spilled out over the garbage bins, scampering off fast when a back porch dog began to howl at their antics, skipping off to the next block if a light in the kitchen went on while they were playing too close to some garage. They'd move on and charge across streets--no notice to the street signs, which might have told them where they were but they couldn't read them anyway. There were three of them and the youngest was only four. They were far away from home and nobody was missing them.

They were frolicking in childish abandon when the squad lights caught them square in the back. They froze for a moment and then ran. Not very fast. There was a pathos in their flight. They were very young, their little legs were very short and they were terrified. They kept looking back to see if it was really the po-lice who were behind them and when they were told to stop, they did.

Cronin and his partner, Knee, got out of the car at Ferdinand and Hamlin. This is not what they normally do. They were not youth

137

officers, beat cops or social workers. Picking up juveniles instead of adult criminals just complicated their night, loaded it up with paper work and took them off the street. They worked gangs. But they'd seen these little shadows darting under the alley lights-- so much smaller than the ones cast by the normal dope dealers, dope runners, and dope lookouts who haunt the night. When their headlights fell on them, they saw these were mere babes.

Where did they come from? There were two eight year olds and a four year old. That's how old they said they were, real straight forward and scared. They were filthy and their shoes had holes. Their socks had disappeared down into their ratty gym shoes. There was crust around their mouths and one of them had a cold. Though they obviously had no sense of time, they said they thought they'd been out playing for a day and a half without going home. They weren't sure. One of the 8 year olds said he lived near-by. And the two others, the other 8 year old and his four year old brother, were staying with him. So, it was okay that they were out. It really was.

"Is that right?" said Cronin. He and Knee led the three up to the one boy's apartment. The one who lived closest. After some time knocking on the door, a woman answered. She was the mother. She was not alarmed to find out he was gone but a little perturbed at being awakened. Yes, this 8 year old was hers but, she said, "I didn't know he went out."

She swatted him on the back of his head when he ducked in the door around her formidable figure.

The other two, they weren't hers and they weren't staying with her. They live, she thought, over a mile away. She didn't know exactly where, maybe Lake and Cicero, but she didn't know their mama. And she didn't know their names. They'd just been hanging around for a couple days, she didn't know how long, really.

Cronin and Knee headed in the car for Lake and Cicero. When they got close, the two boys directed them the rest of the way. It was an apartment building and the only way they knew to get in was up the back porch.

"We don't got no key," said the eight year old from the back seat, where he and his younger brother sat big-eyed, their small legs sticking straight out, not long enough to bend down from the back seat. Cronin and Knee went up the back steps of the building, the kids behind them. There was a party or something going on. They could hear the noise. The back door was locked and that door would get them into the hallway. Their apartment, the boys said pointing, was down the way.

The policemen knocked on the back door. It was ignored. They banged harder with their flash lights and they heard someone yell, "Shut the fuck up!" They shouted "police" and kicked it with their feet. There was a fumbling at the lock.

"Yeah?"

"Po-lice."

"What'chu want?"

"We got some kids here, are these your kids?" The door opened slightly and a man angrily looked out at them. He was drunk.

"Shiiiiit, no. They belong at the end of the hall."

"Then open the door, man, so we can get these kids back home. We found them in an alley."

The man mumbled, glared at the two boys, weaved backwards and pulled the door open with him. The policemen and the two boys walked into the hall which was dark and poorly lit. A woman down the hall poked her head out of an apartment door.

"You their mother?"

"I'm their auntie."

"Where's their mother?"

"She live here, but I ain't seen her in a while. She out. I don't know where she be."

"Well, we found these two boys over at..."

"What the fuck you doing here?" said the drunk man. "You the police and you ain't got a warrant. What the fuck you doing in here. Who you to be stomping in this place, no fucking warrant, these kids bringing the fucking police back with'em, you got no right ..."

"Shut the fuck up!" said Cronin.

The woman just stood there. So did the two boys. They did not run into her arms nor did she open them and offer.

"Is this their home? It's almost 2 in the morning and they were still out running around...."

139

"This be their apartment," she said unconcerned, opening the door wide. The two boys scurried in without looking back.

"How long they been gone?" she asked.

"We don't know. We just found them. Don't YOU know."

"Ain't missed'em," she said.

Then she slammed the door. The two cops could hear her yelling at the kids through the cheap dry wall.

They turned to leave and walked past the drunk man who was now at the open door of his apartment, inside his doorway swearing about the kids, saying something about the police, and how those kids brought the police into the place. How the police had no right, how he wanted to whoop those kids, bringing in the police at this hour of the night, how, when he saw them next, he was gonna...and he was, the little motherfuckers! He was gonna....

The two gang crimes officers walked out on the back porch and headed down the stairs, the sounds of shrieking at their backs . There really was nothing to say. Finally, Cronin said it when they got into the squad car and it was quiet.

"You know," he said, "I don't know if we did these kids a favor."

"NO, CRONIN. I'M A PIMP!"

It is March and all the shadows are grey. The afternoon sky settles grey-blue over the city and stays that way until late. There are no leaves on the trees and all the winter's refuse once hidden under a bed of white snow lies wet and soiled flat, now that the winter cover has melted. They are forgotten things from softer days – a lone roller skate sits crushed in a gutter, a child's mitten still glued to a crack in a sidewalk.

Grey is the color of the lake at this time. Grey are the streets, the trees before they are wetted by rain. Grey is the color of the two flats, the high rises, the sidewalks when there is no sunshine. Grey are the bush branches before they bloom. Grey is the dawn and grey is dusk and grey is the mood of March in Chicago.

It was such a day when Cronin pulled up in his unmarked squad next to a man standing in front of a crumbling two-flat. It was a drug house and the man didn't budge when Cronin called his name or move a muscle in his face when Cronin got out of the car. He was sullen, like the weather, but he wore sun glasses. Dark ones, that hid his eyes. It was drizzling lightly but he wore no raincoat.

"Take off the glasses, Dre. There ain't no sun right now," said Cronin, walking up to him.

Dre took off the glasses and squinted as if the sun was shining. But it was twilight.

"Why are you fucking with me, Cronin?" he asked.

"This is a drug spot and you are a drug dealer, aren't you?" said Cronin, walking up to him. "I want to make sure it is really you."

"I'm not a drug dealer no more," he said. "I'm a pimp."

"No," said Cronin, looking at him square in the face. "You are a drug dealer."

"Maybe I am," he said sullenly.

"Then," said Cronin, "I'm going to have to try to catch ya. That's my job. To clean up the streets."

"Then clean up the streets. Look at'em," said Dre pointing to the garbage lying flush up against the curb. "You going to clean up the street, right?"

"I'm going to clean you off of it if you're dirty, man," said Cronin, reaching down and patting Dre's pants down, starting at the waist and going down to his high tops. "Ain't no garbage dirtier than a dope dealer. This other stuff you can sweep up with a broom."

"What you looking for, Cronin? I ain't got nothing on me."

"Who knows. If not dope, then maybe a gun."

"You know, people can't step outside their homes around here without a gun," said Dre.

"That's because of people like you," said Cronin. "But tonight you don't have a gun. Now ain't that something?"

"I don't need one," said Dre. "I know how to run."

"Well, as long as you sell dope, you better start running," said Cronin, walking back to his car. He started it and headed down the street, into more of the city and the growing grey.

Dre put his shades back on, looked to the left, then the right and then straight ahead...out into his own darkness.

A WINDOW WITH NO VIEW

The kid was lying on his stomach, shot dead and sprawled in a pool of his own warm blood on a bumpy graveled backyard road they call an alley in Chicago. His head was cocked sideways, and his mouth was open, frozen in anguish from the pain of a couple of bullets that caught him in the back. Perhaps by surprise. Or maybe he knew it was coming – and he was running, hoping that in the dark, somebody's aim was not straight.

He was a small time, corner drug hustler, working for someone he admired, probably, or feared, but someone who could pay him in cash and not demand a high school diploma for 8 hours of work. He had a mother somewhere who didn't know yet and some sisters and brothers and probably a teenage girl that was carrying his baby. But this night, barely past the age of 21, without a drivers license or anything in his pocket to identify him, he lay dead in an alley.

Cronin was nearby when the call came in of shots fired. He and Rawski drove in through the alley, past the rear end of empty lots which years ago were backyards where the kids ran through the sprinkler and grandma sat on a kitchen chair on the back porch, watching over them. There was no family life on these lots anymore--not even houses--just dead things and garbage.

Because it was the 11th district, the most violent district in the city, with beat policemen used to gunshots and reacting fast, a squad car was already on the scene. Its blue dome lights were circling eerily in the night, flicking shadows out that scanned the dark. The doors of the police car were open, with the headlights shining straight out and over where the young man lay dead. Their police radio was cracking crisp reports in the autumn air and the two young policemen were bent over the body, running their maglights over him like mine sweepers.

The address was on south Troy street and because Cronin knew a drug dealer named Sharkey lived in an apartment in front of where the body was found, he and his partner went up to the third floor and knocked on the door. Maybe the dead man was one of Sharkey's guys. Then again, maybe he wasn't. Sharkey answered and let them in. But he didn't let on.

"So what's up?" said Sharkey, acting not at all surprised that the law was at his door. And not that interested either, for he promptly sat himself down on a sofa to watch television. He had three buddies with him, all of them slouched down in their chairs, their legs splayed out, intent on the tv set.

"What do you mean, what's up?" said Cronin. "Looked out your window lately?"

"Naw, Cronin, we been sitting here all night watching a movie."

It was a large tv set, more than four feet high, rather like a small movie screen and the sound was set full blast while cars were crashing, people were fighting and men were pulling guns on each other and shooting, Hollywood style. Cronin and his partner asked a few questions of the audience--Sharkey's buddies. One had just gotten out of prison after seventeen years for murder. Another had just finished doing time for manslaughter. The third, a younger one who seemed nervous, was awaiting trial on drug charges. They did not take their eyes off the screen.

"What are you watching this crap for?" asked Cronin.

"Cause it's a good one, Cronin."

"It's all violence and it ain't real," said Cronin.

"Seems real, looks real to me," said one of the men.

"Well if you want to know what's real, look out the back window. You got a dead man lying out there in your alley."

"Don't know nothing about it, Cronin," said Sharkey. He didn't get up and look out the window. Nobody did.

"You didn't hear anything? Any shots fired?"

"Only shots we heard were on TV."

"You got the good life, don't you Sharkey? Big ole tv set half the size of your wall and I bet you paid for it in cash. You and your homies all chilling out watching actors shooting fake bullets and falling fake dead with catsup smeared all over them with background music and some director saying,'Cut' and then they all get up and go for lunch break and fix their make up and you get a thrill out of that shit. That ain't real, Sharkey.

"The real thing is right out there in the alley, lying dead. Don't have to rent a movie to see this shit. It's right there 30 feet away but you don't know nothing, you don't want to know nothing long as it ain't you lying there. You don't give a fuck."

"We're watching a movie, Cronin. No crime in that."

"You're right, Sharkey. No crime in pretend."

Cronin and his partner headed for the door. The four men stayed seated, their butts glued low to the chairs, their eyes focused on a bloody gun fight in the movie. That's how the policemen left them that night--watching tv.

No one ever bothered to ask the dead kid's name.

LUCKY NEVER FINISHED THE PICTURE

There was a body under the white bed sheet, curled up like a frightened caterpillar.

It lay quiet and still until Cronin opened the hospital room door and walked in.

"Lucky, is that you under there?" he asked.

The form didn't answer but it moved. A deformed claw of a hand with wide ridged fingernails emerged from underneath the shroud and clumsily brushed the top of it down to reveal two dark eyes and a nose peeking out.

"Cronie. I knowed it was you when I heard your voice. How'd you know where I was?"

"That's my job, Lucky," said Cronin. "Keeping track of guys like you. I come to say hello and talk to you."

"Man, Cronie, it's good to see you and I never thought I'd say that."

"Do you need anything?" said Cronin.

"I'd like a Snickers bar," said Lucky.

"I'll go get you one. Wait there."

"Not going anywhere, Cronie. Not now, probably not never again."

"You ain't been going nowhere for a long time," said Cronin. "But I'll be back."

"You always said that," said Lucky, chuckling as much as his frail strength allowed. "And you always did come back – showed up when we was trying to duck you."

Cronin went off to the cafeteria on his errand.

So this was Lucky's fate, a ripper, a runner, a player, a burglar and a killer, waiting patiently, curled up in a hospital bed, for his old nemesis to bring him one candy bar.

Lucky Wade, age 36, father of three, never married but already a grandfather, had been shot not once but twice and was paralyzed from the waist down. Lucky was one of the terrible Wade brothers and a member of the notorious Wade family, which consisted of a mother, father and twelve children, eight of them boys. This family, according to Cronin, was the wildest he'd ever seen on the West Side. Every single Wade brother had been shot, two were already dead and Lucky was paralyzed. At one time, every single living Wade son was in an Illinois state prison.

"The devil don't want what he already got," his mother once told Cronin. "He want what he don't got so he got all my sons, including Lucky."

At one time, the Wade family lived at 3422 W. Roosevelt Road, a second floor apartment that, says Cronin, was the only apartment on the West Side that had no locks. Lucky claimed it was so you could get in real fast when you had to, "like when running from the police," and exit from the rear before anyone could catch you. Everyone on the West Side knew where the Wades lived and, so unafraid was the Wade family of any fool who would try to enter their abode, they also had no door knobs. The apartment was a slovenly, crowded, falling down place with grease on the walls a half inch thick, stained mattresses with no sheets anywhere and everywhere, sleeping bodies, mostly children. Crusted oatmeal and bologna sat open on a mungy table that had obviously been there for days. No one had swept the kitchen floor in probably two years. Everything that fell down on it just got ground in and joined the layers of filth that served as a soft and sticky rug.

This is how Lucky Wade grew up.

While Cronin was gone, Lucky lay relaxed and appeared briefly content. Behind his bed, posted on a bulletin board, was a handout from some evangelical group that gleefully roamed the halls of this west side hospital, and the handout stated in bold words, THE END IS NEAR. Sharing the room with Lucky was an old black man who was wired to tubes and machines and lay head back and mouth open and with each breath emitted a brittle rattle that came from deep within, like an old car engine whose pistons were all cracked and broken and couldn't go any further. Lucky said three old men such as he had died in front of him in the last two months.

Cronin returned delivering the candy bar and a tall Styrofoam cup of pop with a bendable straw so Lucky could sip on it while lying flat.

"Hey, Lucky. You got brothers and you got sisters, Don't they bring you anything?"

"They don't bring me nothing," Lucky said. "They don't hardly come see me. Nobody much come but you. How's it going Cronie? I mean out there?"

"It's quieter with some of you Wades gone," said Cronin. "Do you regret any or all of this? The things you've done and the way you are?"

"The way I am? I don't like being like this. You know what, Cronie? I messed up my whole life. My whole life been messed up. I don't blame nobody. I just come through life and didn't know nothing. Lots of things I didn't know, lots of things I never got teached. That's what happened to me. I brought it on myself."

Lucky was in jail when he first heard about Cronin. "I heard about this cop they called Cronie," remembered Lucky. "Everybody knew his name. Then I got out and there was a raid on the place I was staying in. I was in the washroom and I was coming toward the front when the police kicked the door in. When they hit the door they had their guns out and everything. My brother was coming with the key but they didn't wait for him. Everybody was against the wall and Cronie, he came in. I didn't know what he looked like but I just knew who he was because he looked for the heroin under the refrigerator. I never saw that before and I said, 'Yep, that must be Cronie!' They still missed the gun. We threw it out the side window."

Lucky started getting in trouble when he was ten years old, about the time he stopped going to school. He stopped going to school because while he was gone down south one summer to visit his grandmother they moved the school boundaries and he suddenly had to walk across the park and into Roman Saints territory.

"The older boys said I was a Vice Lord, but I was still a little boy. I started getting into fights and I stopped going to school. I never did learn to read in school. My mama got out a little book once and tried to get me to read the words like 'cat,' but I couldn't do it so she got mad and put the book away. After that, when she wasn't around, I sneaked that little book and hid it so that I never had to do that again. I only learned to read in the penitentiary."

Lucky Wade might have been marked as a Vice Lord when he was young, because the neighborhood that he lived in was Vice Lord territory. But the eight Wade brothers became their own gang and were feared. They robbed, burglarized, killed, they even shot each other. The oldest brother was shot and killed by another member of the family in the family's kitchen apartment when he was seventeen. Lucky then became the oldest of the boys. The youngest son, Sherman, was acting dopey on 'Happy Sticks' one day so rather than get a tongue-lashing he was shot by one of his brothers through the left side. Sherman said he bore no grudges and wore his scars proudly. No one in the family called the police or reported the shooting. Sherman spent a month in the hospital, at taxpayer's expense, and moved back home.

Lucky's bad luck may have begun when he quit school, or with the neighborhood he was raised in, or the family he was born into, or the appetizing taste of the streets that seemed liberating, but unseen and undetected, like a carbon monoxide leak, there lurked doom.

Lucky tried a couple of straight jobs, not for long, but he gave it a brief whirl.

Cronin once asked him did he ever have a bank account, and what kind of straight jobs and Lucky responded, "Cronie, I was working downtown in the lobby of a hotel with the bellboys. That's when you take a dustpan and make sure the ashtrays are all clean and everything, right across the street from the John Hancock on Michigan Avenue. I think it was the Continental. Stayed there a long time, about three months. I was too young for that job see, that was for an older man, an older guy who could hustle. In that job you had to have experience if you wanted to hustle and it wasn't just that Cronie. The guy who worked outside, he wore a big hat like a Conservative Vice Lord. A hat with a gray suit, and you had to relieve him for lunch, and man, everybody be putting money in your hand and you're trying to put it in your pocket and trying to park their cars and all sorts of stuff and they're telling you what to do and what not to do out there and I saw all these people and I thought, 'Oh, I got to go.'

"Then Cronie, I got an office job one time, too. At the Urban League. Filing and taking files over to 400 Peoria. How long did I work there? Let's see now ... how many checks did I get? They all stacked up on me. And I bought some nice clothes. I think I got five checks. It seemed like easy money at first, these straight jobs, but it wasn't. Me and one of my brothers, he's in the penitentiary now, bought drugs and him and me were going to sell it and keep turning it over, until we got bigger and bigger packages, right? But we ended up snorting a lot of it and then we wanted to make it strong so that they would come running back to us and buy more and a crowd would build up and then you could cut it back down, but nothing worked right. I got hooked. He didn't get hooked. He's just in the 'Pen' for robbery, but I got hooked."

Thus began the saga of Lucky's shooting others and getting shot himself.

In one shooting, which Cronin knew about, and Lucky talked about with Cronin, he shot and killed the twin brother of a gang member named Junior Ellis. It was a fight over who had the biggest dog. Lucky claimed that the other guy pulled a gun and put it in his face so Lucky pushed his arm away, pulled his own gun and shot and killed him. He claimed in court it was self defense, and he got off.

Thus began Lucky's next foray into violence, with his brother named Eckstein.

When Cronin asked him if Eckstein was named after the singer, Billy Eckstein, Lucky said, "No, Cronin. He wasn't named after no singer. He was named after a genius."

"You mean Einstein?"

"Yeah ... that genius!" said Lucky.

"Eckstein wasn't no genius, was he? The day that you two tried to rob the drug dealers he got killed and you got shot. I didn't see no genius lying in that alley."

Lucky and his brother Eckstein had set out to hold up some drug dealers. They went behind a building to the alley entrance, knocked on the door and the man who answered the door had a machine gun, saw it was two Wade brothers and shot and killed Eckstein. Lucky ran away and returned shortly in a car to come and pick up the body of his brother. At that point, the drug dealers shot Lucky.

It took months for Lucky to recover, which he did partially. He could walk on a cane, barely, but as Lucky told Cronin later, "I couldn't run, Cronie, but I could still drive a car."

And being able to drive was all he needed to go on his next caper. It was going to be the armed robbery of another drug dealer. What Lucky didn't realize was that he was being set up for his own execution. His partner in the planned armed robbery, a man they called Bo Diddley on the street, was the man who was going to do it. And did. But once again, Lucky didn't die. At least right then.

"See, here's what happened that fooled me. I was staying at Ernestine's house and I wanted to do a stickup real bad and I was going in with a rifle and I could drive a car, but I got trapped. We were going to a drug house. We had ski masks and I think it was on a Friday."

What Lucky Wade did not realize was that Bo Diddley had been hired by Junior Ellis to kill him because Lucky had killed Junior's twin brother. And Lucky, still half paralyzed and cocky with a cane, was still stupid enough to plan on committing another armed robbery.

When Bo Diddley got out of the van, he opened the back door, grabbed one of the rifles and shot Lucky directly in the back, leaving him paralyzed from the waist down and with only one partially-functioning arm.

After that, with no hope in sight to ever walk again, rob again, kill again or run the streets again, Lucky read the Bible and spent endless hours in solitude. When he saw Cronin, however, his spirits picked up, his eyes brightened and he still wanted to talk about the street, something that ran in his blood.

"Cronin, you got a gun case on one of my brothers. He'll probably beat that gun case Cronie."

"Lucky, Lucky, Lucky, let me tell you the truth. I don't give a fuck. I gave it my best try. I wrote the best case report I could write on it. If he beats it, he doesn't beat me. He beats the system and I'm just part of it. That's the way I am. I could say the gun was in his coat, but it wasn't. I could say he made a statement that it was his gun, but he didn't. I wrote the case the way it was. It ain't nothing to get excited about, Lucky."

"I know Cronie. That's another thing about you. You're straight up, and everybody knows it."

"Every time a judge throws a case out everybody that's playing and working within the system is a loser," Cronin said. "It's not like I lost the case, me, by myself. This community, the West Side, loses more than anything cause you know, you got people going right back on the street, fucking up the street, shooting dope, shooting people. The system loses. The neighborhood loses. But not for long. What goes around comes around."

"I know Cronin."

"The real losers are the decent people who live there," Cronin said. "If he beats the case, I don't lose, the police department doesn't lose. You all lose."

"You know Cronin, in the joint I learned how to paint. I have very good handwriting and I read the Bible a lot now. I did some paintings and showed it to my father who was a minister and he looked at a book I was making in jail and he looked at it like it was nothing. He didn't make any comment until it was too late but you know, my art is important because I can use my one hand now and there's a lady who comes here and helps me. And Cronin, I'm painting a picture of you. It's a picture of you in the Garden of Eden. I'm going to give it to you some day when I'm done. It's gonna be my present to you. By the way, Cronin. When you come back again ..."

"I will Lucky."

"Could you bring me an Almond Joy, a McDonald's hamburger and a big pop?"

"I'll bring you a double Almond Joy," said Cronin.

"I'll eat one half of it and save the other thinking of you," said Lucky. "And I'm going to finish that picture."

Cronin came again several times and brought him Almond Joys and hamburgers and tall sodas in Styrofoam cups with bendable straws. And then, not long after, some Illinois official notified Cronin that Lucky Wade had fallen sicker and sicker and finally died. No one mentioned any art left behind so Lucky never got to finish the picture. It probably got thrown away.

"I learned very quickly that if you had a Cronin case, you had a good case. He told the truth. He never put a case on a guy."

> – Terry Hake, Former Assistant State's Attorney who went undercover in the Greylord Investigation which led to the indictment of 92 people, including 17 judges, 48 lawyers, 8 policemen, 10 deputy sheriffs, 8 court officials and 1 state legislator.

AND THEN THE JUDGE
LEANED DOWN AND SAID ...

They pulled him over in the 4200 block of west Maple. The man was driving a little funny and smoking a marijuana cigarette. Nothing major, no grand felony, but odd wasn't it, that he was so nervous?

His name was Steve Robinson and when Drozd and Cronin and a third officer riding with them named Joe August searched the car they found a surprise in the glove compartment: $17,000 wrapped in tinfoil. That was a lot of money in the early 1970s.

Robinson wouldn't say where it came from and he wouldn't say where it had been and he pretended like he knew nothing about it.

But, he did make an offer he thought they couldn't refuse. He told them to take the money, it was theirs. They took the money alright, inventoried it and charged Mr. Robinson with bribery.

In court, Robinson showed up with a private attorney and his mother. He pleaded guilty to the charge. The judge, Dan Ryan, apparently in a tolerant mood toward bribery, sentenced him only to probation.

Then mother stood up and announced she wanted the money back for it was her life savings. Cronin found that ridiculous since she was on welfare. The attorney argued on the mother's behalf since without the money he would not get paid. Judge Ryan ordered the officers to hand over the $17,000 in cash. They did and the accused, the mother and the attorney left the courtroom to divvy up the dough.

Astounded at the whole scenario, the policemen stood there for a few moments. And then, the judge leaned down and said quietly to them, "You guys must be crazy."

"It's not us that's crazy," thought Cronin. "It's the Cook County Court system that's crazy when it doesn't take bribery seriously."

POST SCRIPT: A year or two later, Steve Robinson held up a cab driver on the north side and shot and killed him. For that he is serving natural life. And a short time after that, an FBI agent approached Cronin and told him his agency thought the $17,000 might have been part of the loot robbed from a bank down south.

"I'll bet you guys were really tempted by that money," said the agent.

"Not for a second," said Cronin.

Apparently, the FBI man didn't know who he was talking to.

G-MONEY: THE KID WHO LIVED IN THE RAGGEDY ASS BUILDING

Cronin first met G-Money at Homan and Monroe in a three-storied stone building on the southwest corner. It was winter and the sidewalks were icy since they had never been salted or even shoveled. Cronin's partner for the night had already gone upstairs to an apartment where they were selling drugs and Cronin was coming up from the first floor and alone. There was a strong, stocky kid coming down and when he saw Cronin he popped the dope into his mouth. It was an 8-Ball, in other words, an eighth of an ounce of cocaine.

Cronin stood in his way and told him to spit it out. The kid pushed Cronin aside on the stairs. Cronin grabbed him and they wrestled and tumbled down to the first floor level where they both fell to the floor and then rolled down the entrance stairs to the street door, Cronin yelling as usual. When they hit the bottom, Cronin's leg came off. The kid, who was strong but scared, jumped up and ran out the door.

Cronin's partner, hearing the commotion, came down and ran after the kid and, being fleet of foot, caught him. The kid's name was G-Money and he didn't want to go to jail and so he listened to Cronin while he was being talked to back at the station.

"I ain't scared of nothin'," said G-Money, "but I don't like being locked up."

"Then listen to what I'm telling you," said Cronin. "Let's see what you know and then we'll see what I can do for you. And remember, I know more than you think I know."

159

Thus began G-Money's special relationship with Cronin.

He'd heard of Cronin but never met him and he never ever thought, he said, he'd meet Cronin in the way he did, knocking his leg off. No one had ever done that before. He'd heard from a fellow gang member that Cronin was fair. And he said he'd talk if it would keep him out of jail.

"He turned out to be, absolutely, the best informant I've ever had," said Cronin. "He wasn't just smart. He was fearless."

G-Money was an urban buccaneer, a young man who cruised the West Side streets like pirates did the Caribbean. G-Money had no real home. Like a pirate, he traveled from port to port, flying his own pirate flag, hat cocked and a hooded sweatshirt covering much of his face. He knew when to duck, when to bow, when to lay low, when to stand up and hold his own, and where the safe inlets were when the deep waters of the West Side got murky and filled with storm. Survival made him cocky but uncannily wise.

G-Money's father, a minister in East St. Louis, was serving time in a federal penitentiary for dealing drugs. His mother had recently been arrested for beating up the man she lived with. G-Money, though smart, had little education.

"I made it to be a freshman in high school," said G-Money, "but I never went to school long enough to get passed to the next grade. I was a freshman for four years. When my baby sister ended up in my class, I said, 'time to go!'" and at that point he officially disappeared from the Chicago school system.

Unbeknownst to fellow gang members, G-Money agreed that night to work with Cronin as an informant. In the beginning, he may not have been serious but Cronin was. And Cronin meant it. At the same time, word had gotten out onto the street that G-Money had dared to wrestle with Mike Cronin and had knocked off his foot. This made him a hero on the street and a gang leader named Little Keith rewarded him with a $2,500 full length black diamond mink coat and matching hat which G-Money wore like a sultan during the day so he could be seen, but not at night when he would meet secretly with Cronin – although not always on time and not always on the day he was supposed to.

One meeting took place after Cronin had beeped G-Money for two straight days and G-Money had not replied. He finally did and Cronin was furious. When they finally met at their rendezvous, Cronin put him in the back seat and drove him to the lowest level of the police parking lot at Harrison and Kedzie to have a private chat.

The deal had been struck that G-Money would wear a wire and Cronin needed permission from the chief judge to obtain it, and it was dependent on G-Money.

"I was beeping you all day yesterday because I wanted to get that fucking court order," said Cronin. "If we do this right, a lot of people are going to go to jail."

"Listen, Cronin. I've been busy. Look, I'm ready for you now. I got fresh cologne on, just ran out the door with this lotion on ..."

"G-Money, we're not talking about how you fucking smell," said Cronin. "We're talking about what you're going to do. We got a big caper here and we're going to do it, one way or the other. We're going to be on the same team. If we're not, you're going to probably end up in jail and I don't think you'd like that."

"But Cronin, this could all get fucked up, I mean fucked up."

"Now listen," said Cronin. "How old are you, G-Money? Twenty? Well, I've been doing this longer than you've been living on earth. And I never got nobody hurt yet. Now we gotta do what we gotta do. And we're gonna do what we agreed on. And you gotta go down to the chief judge."

"But a lot of my homies are over at 26th Street," complained G-Money. "They'll see me."

"The chief judge is on the ground floor. He's the head of all judges. We go into his chambers, not into a court room. And you do it there. That's it. And if you don't show up and you get goofy on me again, you better leave the state because we're going to be looking for you and the gang members we've been talking about are going to be looking for you."

"So I go where again? 26th and California."

"You know the place, G-Money," said Cronin. "And you'll fit right in. It's right next to Narcotics Court. You being there is nothing unusual, not like you being seen at church and people saying, 'What the fuck is G-Money doing at church? They'll just see you near the Narcotics Court which is Branch 25. You talk to the judge in private, the order gets signed, it gets sealed, that's it and we get to work."

"I hear you Cronin, but it still seems like it'll all get fucked up."

"You're not going to get fronted off. You're not. And if we do it right, these guys will all be arrested and convicted. Do you believe me?"

"Well, it's fucked up now," said G-Money. "So I might as well do it with you, and I don't want to go to jail, so I guess I'm going to do it your way. I'm ready, you watch, you'll be calling me back."

"Okay, G-Money. We're on the same wave length, but if I beep you and I don't hear from you, I won't have time for any more shit. I'm too old to chase you around G-Money, but I'll sweat you like a motherfucker and don't think I won't remember you. You got it?"

"I got it Cronin. I'll see you on Monday."

"Now where do you want me to drop you off?"

"I'll show you Cronin," said G-Money, and he directed Cronin to a run-down old apartment building.

They arrived and Cronin turned and looked back to G-Money. "This ought to be interesting," Cronin said. "You living in this raggedy ass building?"

"Yeah, this raggedy ass building where my girlfriend lives."

"Okay, G-Money, this is it man. We gotta get going. I'll see you then, and don't wear your hat like a banger."

"I know Cronin, it's a habit ..."

"Well, change the habit. Now you ain't going to go to the joint and you ain't going to get hurt, I promise you. Do you believe me when I tell you that?"

"Un-huh. I hear you."

G-Money exited the car and Cronin drove away.

POST SCRIPT: G-Money worked with Cronin for over two years. G-Money did wear a wire and sometimes, later, referred to Cronin as his father. He personally testified in several cases, with the gang members in the court room. His work resulted in fifteen arrests and convictions, mostly of the leadership of the Vice Lords gang, the most powerful gang on the West Side.

But the kid who lived in the raggedy assed building refused to be intimidated by any of them. He was given money not once, but twice, to leave town so that he could be safe, but he never left. The first time, Cronin and an IRS agent took him to the Greyhound Bus Station where he was set to go to Alabama, where his grandmother lived. But it was a small, nothing changing but the weather type of town. No street life, no energy, no action, no snappy ladies, no playing until 4 a.m., no ripping and running.

Cronin gave him $500, and the IRS agent gave him $1,000, and they handed him a bus ticket. Cronin offered to walk him to the bus but G-Money said no. That would front him off, being seen with Cronin, so they watched him walk away toward the buses. Cronin had told him to call him or beep him when he got to Alabama. Cronin never heard from him.

Then he got word from the street that G-Money was spotted on the South Side. And finally, when G-Money needed money, he beeped Cronin and suggested they work the Nigerians. That plan didn't work the same. G-Money eventually went to Indianapolis, was arrested for robbery and sentenced to the only thing he feared – prison.

"At this stage," said Cronin, "I have no idea if he's alive or dead, but he's the best darned informant, and the smartest one, I ever met."

"I'LL TAKE THE STREETS ANY DAY"

There is a fine line one must walk to be a street cop on the West Side. A balancing act between toughness and fairness and the ability to enforce the law but not be brutal. You have to learn not to take things personally and to play by the rules when the criminals don't have to or don't want to.

It takes time to know the neighborhood you work in better than the one you live in and to know more than the people you're interviewing but not let them know you know what you know.

It takes time and Cronin put in the time. It takes tenacity and stubbornness and an unwillingness to give up, like a bulldog, and Cronin became an old bulldog. He never gave up and he never burned out. It never bothered him going out alone at night, or venturing where few policemen would go without backup, sneaking into a derelict old hovel filled with rats to watch drug dealing across the street, or venturing into the hallways of public housing buildings where the lights were blasted out, or stopping a caravan of three gangster cars alone and searching them by himself.

Perhaps because of what he endured in Vietnam he figured there was nothing left to fear. He exuded confidence but not recklessness. On the street, that was noticed and respected.

Many myths grew around the name Cronie, some true, many not.

One gang member claimed Cronin limped because he shot him in the foot.

Cronin never limped, he listed to the left when he'd been on his feet for hours. And for at least two decades, most policemen never

165

even knew he was missing a foot. Cronin never talked about it and they never asked.

Cronin never married. He was wed to the job, married to the street. He drove old cars, one of which he called "George," and still does.

He lives in a bungalow with two pear trees in a very small backyard. In the winter time, he shovels the sidewalks of the two old ladies who live on either side of him. They'd been friends of his Irish mother.

All the little notebooks he kept in his left shirt pocket, filled with old license plate numbers, addresses, street names, are stacked in boxes heaped in piles upstairs in his attic in case he might still need them. All the clothes he's owned since high school and never thrown out have crowded up the basement floor.

He was constantly teased by fellow officers about his outdated and unsophisticated wardrobe. Even gangbangers, wise-assing, would say, "Cronin, my shoes are worth more than what you got on."

And Cronin would respond, "Yeah, but I didn't steal it."

Cronin's reputation grew over the years, on the street and inside the department, to the bosses downtown, where he became known as a man who knew what he was doing out there and knew what he was talking about. He was a man who ventured where few middle class people ever went and saw things most Americans never see.

Vince Lane, who at one time headed the Chicago Housing Authority, called Cronin in and offered him the position of heading the CHA police. Cronin wisely deferred.

A year or two later, Mayor Richard M. Daley called Cronin in and asked if there was something else on the police department he would like to do. There was no mention of the role that the mayor's father played in giving Cronin the chance to become a police officer. It was quietly understood. Cronin modestly demurred and said he was happy being a gang crime specialist and working on the street. He might have been the only person who ever left the mayor's office without asking for a thing.

"I'll take the streets any day," Cronin told a friend.

When Phil Cline became police superintendent in October, 2003, he made an unprecedented move. He took this man named Mike

Cronin, who had never even made sergeant, and promoted him to an exempt position as the commander of the department's Gang Crimes unit. A year later, he promoted Cronin again to the position of Deputy Chief to command not just Gang Crimes but the Narcotics Unit as well – the two hottest and most elite units in the city. And violent crimes due to gangs and drugs fell dramatically. Although not a sitting-behind-the-desk kind of policeman, he offered in that new job experience and leadership. And sometimes, inspiration.

In the autumn of 2006, the gang unit had a confrontation with gang members on a west side street. Police surveillance revealed that the armed and masked men in a car were on their way to assassinate several opposing gang members. Cronin was there and drove his squad in front of their car to prevent them from escaping the scene.

There was a shootout then with police in which two gang members were killed and one wounded. Wounded also was a young Chicago policeman who was taken to the hospital and told his finger would have to be amputated.

Police Superintendent Cline visited him and the young officer asked, "Will I be able to come back on the job? Will I be able to come back on gangs?"

"Sure you will," said Cline. "Look at your Deputy Chief, Mike Cronin. He's only got one foot."

POST SCRIPT: In the fall of 2006, Mayor Daley called Cronin in one more time as Cronin was facing mandatory retirement because he'd reached the age of 63. Did he want to still keep working, but as a civilian, as an advisor to the gang and narcotics units and as an expert, sharing the knowledge of what he'd learned over the decades? The answer was yes.

So, back Cronin now goes, on the street, doing life.

IN GRATITUDE TO:

Kitty Hanrahan Dawson, Patty Mulvaney and all those who spoke frankly about Michael Cronin and his early life.

Mike Fryer who provided the cover photograph.

The incredible help from former police officer Kim Anderson.

The patience and support of my husband, Leonard Aronson.

And to Dr. Samuel Southwick who has a wonderful place in Jackson, Wyoming, we call "Uncle Sam's Cabin," where one can ponder and think and work on a book such as this.

Printed in the United States
70056LV00006B/119